UNSUNG HEROES OF THE ROYAL CANADIAN AIR FORCE

AMAZING STORIES

UNSUNG HEROES OF THE ROYAL CANADIAN AIR FORCE

Incredible Tales of Courage and Daring During World War II

HISTORY

by Cynthia J. Faryon

PUBLISHED BY ALTITUDE PUBLISHING CANADA LTD.
1500 Railway Avenue, Canmore, Alberta T1W 1P6
www.altitudepublishing.com
1-800-957-6888

Extreme care has been taken to ensure that all information presented in
this book is accurate and up to date. Neither the author nor the
publisher can be held responsible for any errors.

Publisher	Stephen Hutchings
Associate Publisher	Kara Turner
Editor	Jill Foran

We acknowledge the financial support of the Government
of Canada through the Book Publishing Industry Development
Program (BPIDP) for our publishing activities.

Altitude GreenTree Program
Altitude Publishing will plant twice as many trees as were used
in the manufacturing of this product.

National Library of Canada Cataloguing in Publication Data

Faryon, Cynthia J., 1956-
Unsung heroes of the Royal Canadian Air Force / Cynthia J. Faryon

(Amazing stories)
Includes bibliographical references.
ISBN 1-55153-977-2

1. Canada. Royal Canadian Air Force--Biography. 2. World War, 1939-
1945--Aerial operations, Canadian. 3. World War, 1939--1945--Personal
narratives, Canadian. 4. Airmen--Canada--Biography. I. Title. II. Series:
Amazing stories (Canmore, Alta.)
D792.C2F37 2003   940.54'4971'0922   C2003-911126-1

Printed and bound in Canada by Friesens
2 4 6 8 9 7 5 3 1

Cover: Spitfires in flight
Reproduced courtesy of British Columbia Aviation Museum

To all the heroes of World War II,
and their amazing stories.

A map of western Europe as it looks today.

Contents

Prologue

The drizzle in Victoria, British Columbia, fogs the windows and makes the road slick. My Chevy van lunges forward, carrying me to adventure, to a dip into the past that will stand sharply in my memory.

The driveway to the West Coast home is steep, and a grey haired gentleman in his 80s meets me at the door with a smile. I've been told he is a hero, but to me he simply looks like someone's father, or grandfather.

"Hi, Cynthia," he says, shaking my hand, "I'm Ken Moore."

His house is warm and welcoming, filled with rich fabric and wood. There is a magnificent window in the living room that reveals a breathtaking valley view.

Ken sits on a couch across from me, and next to him is a plastic bag filled with photos, newspaper clippings, and letters — the standard sort of material that is saved, cherished, and placed into scrapbooks that will serve to depict a life lived.

Usually collections like these are given to me by

family members anxious to recapture a life after a loved one has passed. But in this case, the man whose life we are here to talk about is sitting right in front of me. Showing the scars of battle in his expressive eyes, he's ready to share his story.

Leafing through his collection of memorabilia, I discover a citation signed by King George VI. "Not many of those in existence," Ken says proudly, "and here, look, a photo of my crew." He rattles off their names, drawing attention to the mascot sitting front and centre. "Dinty" is the mascot's name; he is a stuffed panda in full air force battle dress.

Ken's voice cracks with emotion. "We were never apart you know. Commissioned and non-commissioned officers alike, we ate, drank, played, flew, and even bunked together. It was against regulations, but they listened when I told the higher-ups it had to be that way. I swear it was the only reason we survived.

"The RAF thought the Canadians were young, high-spirited, and too un-disciplined, yet they still extended to us an undefined kind of respect. We were farm boys, many of us, and we were given opportunities that would never have happened if not for the war. Prairie boys, some of us poorly educated, and there we were rubbing shoulders with the likes of royalty, as well as military and political giants."

Prologue

He sighs and fights the tears that are gathering in his eyes. Then his voice gives out and he looks away to regain control. He has a strength and dignity that eludes description as he gazes out the window, and back 60 years.

"The emotion catches me unawares," he whispers. "It floods, and suddenly I'm back there. No one prepared us for that kind of memory. And I know I'm not the only one who experiences the flood. I went to England for the 50th anniversary of D-Day. Liverpool accommodated almost three million visitors during that time, and we all experienced that powerful flood. It seemed to catch us all by surprise. I guess it permitted us a time of mourning together.

"We were just kids, you know. We didn't know we were doing anything special. We were simply putting one foot in front of the other and hoping we survived."

The interview lasts an hour, and covers a period in Canadian history that changed the shape of the world.

Chapter 1
First Mission of a Rear Gunner

s he stands outside the air force hut, Larry Cramer looks southeast in the direction of Holland and Germany. It is evening and the trees are boldly silhouetted against the darkening sky. The world seems to be losing clarity with the coming of twilight.

"Peaceful," Larry thinks to himself, "and it's almost flight time."

Larry is at the Elvington Air Force base in York, England. He and the rest of his aircrew are about to embark on their freshman sortie, and while excited to be officially part of the war effort, Larry feels his stomach doing cartwheels. He takes a deep pull on his cigarette and blows the smoke into the air pensively. The time has come at last to set off somewhere into the unknown, to seek out targets, and to help the Allies win this war. The date is May 23, 1943, and the targets are the munitions factories in Dortmund, Germany.

The aircrew's Halifax bomber (often called a kite or a heavy) is fit for action. The bomber's call letter is "E," for *Edward*, and it stands waiting on the field in a parking bay close to dispersal. *Edward* has had some maintenance done, and Larry's skipper, Pilot Officer Ron Pritchard, has already taken the kite up for a test flight.

Larry takes one more pull on his cigarette and stomps it out on the English soil. For a moment he thinks of his folks back in Arborfield, northern Saskatchewan. Right about now, Pa would be milking the cows and Ma would be getting the darning out. If he were at home, he'd be cleaning stalls and brushing the horses. But he's a long way from home.

After briefing, there is a short reprieve and then preparation begins in earnest. Pilots and navigators consult together, studying the flimsies provided by intelligence. The flimsies list the night's colours for aircraft resins and Very recognition lights, which are placed on the wings of the Allied aircraft to help with identification. The lights are changed for every operation, as is the code word for aborting the mission.

After his pre-flight meal, Larry makes his way back to the barracks to get his personal things in order. He takes a moment to write a letter home, puts his effects together with a list of future ownership, and adds what's left of his pay in the envelope with the letter. Going through this, Larry feels like he's already died, and knows that once he takes off into the night, the world will carry on as if he never existed. He feels lonely, and he tries to ignore the macabre thoughts running through his mind as he prepares to kill and to be killed.

Transport finally arrives to take the crews to the hangars. The men silently pile into the vehicles and bump their way out to the airfields, where they collect their flight maps and receive last minute instructions. When the crews get to the hangars, Larry sees navigators working around a large table with topographical maps and plotting charts. His nervousness has left an emptiness in the pit of his stomach, and he walks through the hangar feeling haunted.

Moments later, Larry slips on his Mae West and adjusts it for comfort, checking that it's reasonably intact and liable to inflate properly if his luck runs out and his "ass gets a dunking," as the skipper likes to say. Grabbing his helmet, Gee board, maps, and flashlight, Larry tucks a bulky parachute under one arm and heads

Five minutes before take off. Jimmy Coles is on the far left of the
picture, Pilot Ron Pritchard is wearing the cap, and Larry Cramer
is second from the right.

outside to wait for the transportation out to the kites. He
feels a slight chill in the air and thinks of how cold it will
be at 18,000 feet.

As Larry waits with the rest of the men, the padre
hands out the flying rations, as well as the emergency
rations and escape kits. The doctor then offers caffeine
pills to anyone who wants them. Larry puts a couple in
his pocket, and turns his collar up against the stiff

breeze. He can't imagine needing the pills, but figures it's better to have them on hand just in case.

Soon the men are scrambling into the transport vans, relieved to be moving again instead of waiting and wondering. The navigators hug their bags of equipment while Larry clutches his parachute and the 60-pound panniers of ammunition for his guns. As the vans progress, each crewmember is dropped off at his dispersal point with shouts of "keep your bottoms down and heads up chaps," and then, "we'll see you for tea."

Finally, Larry and his fellow crewmembers are dropped off at their aircraft. They stand beside the kite with mounting unease, smoking their last cigarettes and doing their best to look nonchalant. Every member of the aircrew is conscious that this is his freshman operation. They're anxious to go, but none of them want the ground-crew boys to see their excitement and nervousness.

Suddenly, flares signalling the Stand by Stations command are shot from the tower. Larry climbs into the Halifax, manoeuvres around the bomb load, and squeezes through the fuselage to his position in the rear turret, almost directly above the tail. He hangs his parachute on the hook outside the entrance to the compartment and takes his seat inside. The height restriction for a rear gunner's compartment is six feet. Larry is six feet and half an inch, leaving no extra space.

As he settles into his compartment, Larry double-checks his ammunition and oxygen supply, tests the swivels, and cranks up the intercom. His flight suit is heated, but Larry knows he will be battling to stay warm once they are airborne.

One by one, the seven crewmembers confirm their readiness over the intercom. Then there's a pregnant pause as they feel the kite hesitate. Thunk. The chorehorse connector sockets into position, supplying the force to turn the four 1480-horsepower Rolls-Royce Merlin 22 engines. The ground crew hooks up the booster battery assembly to each engine in turn. A muffled high-pitched whine begins as the port propeller on engine one begins to turn. Hesitantly, almost reluctantly, the engine coughs and hiccups as wisps of smoke rise from the exhaust. After a few turns, the Merlin fires to a rumbling thunder. Then engine two fires, followed by three and four, all leaping to life without hesitation. The Halifax bomber shudders and trembles beneath Larry like a dragon on the verge of flight. The giant is awake, and the four propellers are spinning so quickly that they're nothing more than a smudge against the skyline.

Larry's excitement is building. Once more, before it's too late, he runs a gun check and then bends forward to latch and secure the turret hatch. The kite is throbbing with the unleashed power of the piston engines, and he can feel the vibrations from the rest of the squadron kites, all vying for their piece of the asphalt. Above the crew, the bomber stream from the other air bases across England is forming with a deafening roar.

It's dark in the rear turret compartment. Larry pulls on his leather helmet, which has goggles and chin straps. The helmet covers his ears, muting the sounds of the strange world around him. The relative quiet is a welcome relief, but it adds to his feeling of isolation in the turret. For the next five and a half hours Larry will be alone with four .303 Browning machine guns as his only companions.

Through the intercom, Larry hears the skipper report to the tower that they are ready for takeoff. Bracing himself, he takes a deep breath. When the okay comes down, the skipper, Pilot Officer Pritchard, signals to the ground crew, who pull the wheel chocks away from the tires and move clear. Pritchard studies the control column, swings the rudder pedals left then right, rechecks the brakes, and runs the engines to the upper limits. Satisfied that everything is in working order, he pulls the two throttle levers all the way back and works the rudders with his feet. The Merlins shift from a skull-splitting whine to a low rumble as the Halifax lumbers forward. Members of the ground crew look at Larry and give him the thumbs up. He returns the signal on behalf of the rest of the crew. Then, the engine noise increases sharply once again as the kite turns to port, picks up speed, and pulls out of the parking bay. The colossal metal bird lumbers along the tarmac to the downwind end of the airfield, lining up at the starting hut.

The skipper's voice crackles over the intercom, "All set? Have we said our piece, then?" One by one, the crewmembers acknowledge their readiness by raising their right thumbs and proclaiming, "Aye, Skipper."

It's completely dark now, and Larry prepares himself for take off. He is seated in a backward position. He doesn't mind travelling backwards once he's up in the air, but the initial sensation of lift off always makes him feel uneasy.

As the kite arrives at the takeoff point, it stops at a right angle to the runway for the final engine run-up. Pritchard engages 30 degrees of flap just as the flashing green light on the windscreen at the hut beside the port wing switches to steady. This light tells the crew the previous plane has cleared the strip and their kite is next to go. Larry's heart catches in his throat. This isn't training. This is the real thing.

The sound of the engines builds into a battle cry of power and the port throttles are pushed ahead to counteract the torque. The Halifax shudders to escape its locked brakes, and the wind from the propellers rushes into the aircraft.

The roaring of the engines subsides as the brakes are released. Pritchard keeps the aircraft stationary until he has enough power to obtain rudder control. He then advances the throttles to fully open and hands them over to the engineer, who holds them steady, leaving the pilot's hands free for the control column. The plane speeds up, and then swings sideways when the torque of the propellers catches a slight crosswind. The cockpit crew barely feels the slide, but to Larry, who sits almost directly over the tail wheel, the sensation of whiplash is intense.

Adding to Larry's discomfort is the shaking and rattling of metal on metal as the kite strains and pitches from side to side. He is helpless to do anything but hang on to what he can — including his pre-flight meal. The live ammunition jostles and clinks ominously in the fuselage, the turret sways and vibrates, and the kite barrels forward, straining for the sky. Finally, an almost imperceptible change in altitude registers in the pit of Larry's stomach. As the tail lifts up, the shift is more palpable. Pritchard pulls back on the control column and the kite is off the ground, pushing upwards and forwards between the white streaks of light lining the airstrip, one on either side. There is a final thump as the wheels bounce once after finding air, and Larry watches the last of the lights slide beneath him and away. Rising against the headwind, the bomber labours steadily into the blackness above.

Out of habit, Larry searches for other planes. Looking above, below, starboard, and port, he sees Halifaxes, Lancasters, and Whitleys. Together, these planes make up a massive force of bombers in the stream. In all, 826 aircraft are assembling into formations for this raid on the city of Dortmund. Moving together like a flock of starlings in a ballet of death, the planes head for the English Channel and the waiting continent.

The first faint wisps of low cloud fly past Larry's bubble, and all at once the plane is enveloped in a thick, grey mist. He feels a double thump somewhere beneath and behind him as the landing gear locks into place. The aircraft wobbles slightly as it continues to climb, heavy with full fuel tanks and over 13,000 pounds (nearly 6000 kilograms) of bombs in its belly. A thin sheen of ice forms on the upper surface of the wings, glistening in reflected red and green. The intercom is silent as all who have a window are gazing intently out into the night, watching for enemy or friendly planes that may get too close. Now and again, Larry catches sight of the exhaust flames from the other bombers, and his stomach settles down. It's comforting to know that he and the rest of the crew are not alone.

The skipper levels the heavy aircraft at 18,000 feet and cruises at 330 km/h.

It's very cold in the turret — Larry's heated suit and mittens are barely keeping him warm. Every few minutes he wiggles in his seat and flexes his toes to make sure they're still awake. As the bomber nears enemy territory, its external lights are extinguished.

At the unseen Heligoland turning point, the plane heads south, crossing the enemy coast that is somewhere beneath them but totally obscured by cloud cover. So far, there has been no challenge to their intrusion, but each crew member has a gut feeling that it won't be quiet for much longer. Somewhere up ahead, the pathfinders are marking the way, and the fighter escort is preparing to engage anyone who stands in the path of the Allied force. Finally, after an hour and three quarters of flying time, they are closing in on the target area.

In the complete blackness, Larry can barely make out the shapes of the nearby bombers; they are mere shadows, revealing only the slightest glimmer of grey metal in the moonlight. Larry's hands are icy, but they are sweating. He feels his fingers cramping, but he can't take his gloves off to rub them; the equipment in the turret is too cold and his bare skin would stick to it. His eyes hurt from combing the skies for the first glimpse of trouble.

First Mission of a Rear Gunner

Suddenly, Larry hears the crew's mid-upper gunner, Jimmy Coles, whisper into the intercom. Jimmy sees the flash of tracer bullets, indicating fighter activity, not too far up ahead. Larry swivels around in his turret and notes the blue searchlights quartering the sky. Some of these searchlights are flitting about randomly in small groups, but others are concentrated in cones consisting of 20 or more lights. One of these cones has a Lancaster bomber pinned to the sky while red bursts of heavy flak from German anti-aircraft guns explode all around. The Lancaster dives immediately and directly at the blue light, feigning a move in one direction then quickly turning in the other. The pilot is swift, and very lucky. The searchlights scatter and then move on to other targets, ones that are not as fast.

Everywhere Larry looks is the bump and flash of flak, and the *Edward* is flying right into the thick of it. Below the heavy, the ground is lit with lines of reconnaissance flares. As the bombers up ahead drop their load and climb roaring into the sky, the target is crisscrossed with streaks of white and flashes of red, where fires have started. Larry tears his eyes away from the action below to keep a lookout for enemy fighters coming in from behind. With all the lights, flashes, and explosions, he's glad the Very lights on Allied planes are obvious, because his trigger finger twitches whenever a fighter advances. Every nerve and muscle in his body is alert and ready.

As the Halifax nears the drop site, flares, gun flashes, streams of flak, and the ever-present searchlights all vie for Larry's attention. Feeling confused and overwhelmed, he fights his panic and gives the pilot directions that will help the crew to avoid the dangers surrounding them. Larry's hands are at the ready, his eyes are constantly scanning, and his mind is travelling faster than the kite. Everywhere he looks there are explosions; planes carrying friends and allies are shot to pieces and plunging helplessly towards the ground.

It's not the fear of dying that plays tricks on Larry's eyes and has his nerves jumping. Instead, it's the responsibility that comes with his job. His guns — his four .303s — won't be used to gain ground or to shoot men in defence of his life alone. Larry is responsible for protecting the lives of his crewmates while the kite forges ahead to the target and drops 13,000 pounds of high explosive and incendiary bombs on the enemy below.

Larry dares not let his eyes fail him during the mission, for he knows that if he were to make just one mistake, he would not be the only one to suffer. If he blinks and misses a Junkers, if he says "corkscrew port, Skipper" when he should have said starboard, or if he gives a direction a fraction too soon or a split second too late, the aircrew could all die and he would be to blame.

Larry's thoughts are broken by the sound of the intercom. He hears the bomb aimer tell the navigator to flip the master switch, and the pilot to open the bomb doors, while he sets his selector switch to release all the bombs together. They commence the attack of the target with a steep dive from 9800 feet, break cloud at 1200 feet, and let go of the bombs.

Instantly, alarms begin to sound in Larry's ears. There's a hang-up and the bombs can't clear the doors. Larry tries to ignore the mayhem over the intercom and focuses his eyes on the sky around him. Flak is exploding all around them, the searchlights are raking the air in search of sitting ducks, and his kite is fully loaded — a ticking time bomb.

Larry's knuckles turn white from tension as he grips his guns hard and sits forward, straining to see. The hair on the back of his neck stands up, and suddenly he can smell the enemy coming at him — but from where? Yes, there it is, a Junkers 88 is heading straight for him, cannons ready. Larry quiets his breathing, waits until he's sure it's too late for the enemy pilot to pull up and out, then yells into the intercom, "Hun, Skipper, 10 o'clock, corkscrew port!" Pritchard manoeuvres the plane and the Halifax disappears from range just as the Jerry fires.

The Jerry's mind is focused on the kill and he isn't prepared for the heavy's dodge. Larry's timing is perfect. The Junkers' guns fly a stream of wasted ammunition right where Larry had been. Then the enemy plane corrects its course and attempts to follow the heavy bomber's gyrations.

"Starboard, Skipper, and dive!" Larry hangs on as he feels the fully loaded bomber groan and whine with the violent evasive manoeuvres. A rivet pops out of the metal plating above his head and pings across the rear turret. The whole crew prays that their kite holds together.

"For God's sake, Larry," the mid-upper gunner swears at him from his perch, "I can't get him in my sights. Shoot already!" Larry takes a deep breath and calms himself. Continuing to shout manoeuvres, he calculates where the Junkers 88 will appear next and prays that his instructions are timed for when the enemy is inside the attacking curve. This will force the Junkers into a steeper turn, and if Larry shoots right into the space that the Halifax has just vacated, the enemy aircraft will fly right into Larry's bullets.

Larry squeezes the triggers — "Raaataataaaaaatat" — and the bullets race away like a deadly string of beads. The Junkers 88 is hit, and shrapnel flies in all directions as the tip of one of its wings explodes. What's left of the enemy aircraft plummets towards the ground, trailing flames and smoke as the cloud cover obscures its descent. None of the aircrew can see a parachute, and because of the thick smoke and flak, they cannot confirm the plane is actually downed. Nevertheless, Larry knows he got the Jerry.

But his elation is short-lived. Out of the corner of his eye he sees a Lancaster, tail section gone, twirling down to the ground below like an autumn leaf. Crewmembers are falling out of the Lancaster's wounded belly — some with parachutes opening, and others without. Then a Halifax is hit, and yet another.

Larry's bomber comes around to attack the target again. The bomb aimer calls directions to the skipper. This is their first mission, and they know they could just fly home and jettison their load, but none of the crew wants that. They all want their freshman mission to be recorded as a success. The men pray that the hang-up has been reversed so they can dive in, drop their load, and get out of there.

"Right, right-steady-left-steady-steady-steady... bombs gone!" The bombs pepper the air behind them, seeming to hover in a deathly quiet above the target area lit by flares, flak, and flames. Larry watches as the bombs hit their mark, sending clouds of smoke and debris high into the sky. This explosive action automatically opens the shutter on the plane's fixed camera and releases the flash bomb. Pritchard flies the kite straight and level until the camera is finished taking photos of the target sight, all the while keeping close watch on the flak and anti-aircraft guns. Photos are secondary to the safety of his kite, but without the pictures, the crew may not be credited with the trip.

Once the photos are taken, the skipper sticks the kite's nose down in a shallow dive, builds up speed in the four Merlins, corkscrews and climbs aggressively away from the target, and banks left for home.

The Halifax has successfully dropped its load of bombs on the target, and the photos can confirm it. The *Edward* is one of 12 bombers that left Elvington with Flight A to join with the 825 other planes from all over Britain. Of the 12, only 6 returned, and it wasn't the flak, the searchlights, or the enemy aircraft that kept the returning crews on their toes during the long and lonely flight home. It was the visions of exploding planes, blown out cockpits, and smoking black holes where the gunner usually sits. It was the memory of bombers and fellow fighters falling aimlessly from the air like the dead leaves of autumn. And it was the knowledge that yet again, they had friends who were no more.

There is nothing Larry and his crewmembers can do for the men who were shot down but put Xs on the squadron photos under the young faces of the fallen;

fresh, youthful faces of men who ate, drank, laughed, and joked with Larry and the others before their mission, but who will now remain forever young.

* * *

Flying Officer Lawrence George Cramer was awarded the Distinguished Flying Cross for this mission. He successfully completed 38 missions as a rear gunner with the Royal Canadian Air Force. He died in 1988 in Duncan, British Columbia.

Chapter 2
Taken Prisoner

loyd Kidd takes off his uniform and pulls on a dark blue turtleneck. He then dons his battle dress shirt and trousers, and slips wool socks over his feet for added warmth. The air-force issue overalls, which zipper from the right ankle to the left shoulder, are set aside. He'll put those on after he visits the latrine. Lloyd makes sure he uses the toilet before each operation. Undoing the zippers and buttons of his overalls to relieve himself at 18,000 feet in the frigid cold is a nasty experience that is rarely repeated.

After visiting the toilet, Lloyd steps into his overalls, then pulls a pair of leather gauntlets over his silk gloves.

The gauntlets extend past his wrists and will help to keep his hands warm during the flight. Lloyd reminds himself once again that while he's in the air he must not remove his gloves to use the flight instruments. If he does, his fingers will stick to the frozen metal. The cold in the aircraft rivals the winters back home in Saskatchewan.

Lloyd chuckles to himself, remembering that one winter, when he was just seven years old, he'd tried to open the latch on the gate at home with his mouth because he had thought it was too cold outside to take his mittens off. Of course, his lips had quickly stuck to the cold metal, and his mother had had to pour a pitcher of warm water over the latch so that he could free his lips without pulling off the skin. She'd been laughing while she did it. Lloyd's own smile widens at the memory. After a moment, he shakes himself out of his reverie and continues with his preparations. Usually he tries not to think of home.

Almost done dressing, Lloyd steps into his pair of black flying boots. These are nothing more than stout walking shoes with suede and lamb's wool uppers extending up over the calves for warmth. In a small pocket inside the upper boot, Lloyd stores the compass and knife that the Royal Air Force provides to each of the aircrew in case of a bail out behind enemy lines. The knife is for slashing away the knee extensions off the boots, providing more mobility for cross-country hiking.

Searching his pockets, Lloyd throws away any evidence that might assist an enemy interrogator in the event that he is shot down and taken prisoner. He then makes sure that he has his special pencil, also RAF issue. The pencil twists apart below the pink eraser, revealing a small map of occupied Europe with escape routes marked. Lloyd slips a picture of his family into the New Testament he received when he first joined the air force and tucks the Bible into his overalls pocket. If one of these items doesn't help him stay alive, perhaps another one will.

Lloyd Kidd is a wireless operator/air gunner (W/AG) posted with No. 78 Squadron at Middleton St. George, England. It's the night of October 2, 1942, and there is a bomber raid scheduled for Krefeld, Germany.

This is Lloyd's 21st sortie, but for some reason it doesn't feel like a routine run. Taking extra time, Lloyd puts his things in order, tidies his sleeping area, and throws out what he doesn't want prying eyes to see. He writes a letter home and leaves the envelope on his bed, sealed and ready for delivery in case he doesn't make it back.

As he walks out of the barracks, the door to the building closes behind him with a hollow thud. Though the sound shakes him, Lloyd continues walking. He heads for the parachute room, where his chute is checked for safety. As it turns out, the chute is too wet to be useable, and he is issued a dry one. Stamped on the outside of the loaner parachute are the instructions "Return in 48 hours." Lloyd takes these orders as a good omen.

Unfortunately, his optimism doesn't last long. Right before takeoff, the Gee (aircraft radar) malfunctions and has to be removed. Already 20 minutes behind schedule, the crew realizes there is no time to replace the unit, even though flying without it will make the kite a blind target for night fighters. Resigned to the problem, the crew sits tight as their plane climbs into the darkened sky. On this particular night, Lloyd is flying as air gunner.

The journey to the target is tense, and the crew is still half an hour off the bombsite when a Junkers 88 swoops down out of nowhere and nails the kite with both guns before anyone sees him coming. A stream of incendiary bombs flies through the air and hits both the starboard engines. The kite catches fire, and all power to the craft's interior is cut off, as are the hydraulics for Lloyd's turret. The intercom is dead, leaving no means for communicating evasive action to the pilot. As Lloyd watches the smoke billow from the two burning engines, the pilot orders the crew to abandon the aircraft. Lloyd obeys and bails backwards from the turret at 15,000 feet.

His descent is uneventful until he hits a tree and falls the last 10 feet to the hard ground below. He buries his chute quickly, managing to smile once again at the 48-hour warning written on its side. Cutting away his uppers, he extracts the escape kit from his pencil and leaves the landing site at a run.

Hours later, right after the sun comes up, Lloyd finds shelter in a bluff and falls into a restless sleep. He's woken up by the sound of two children playing nearby, and spends an uneasy couple of hours hoping they don't discover his hiding place. Once they leave, he dozes fitfully again, waiting for darkness to fall before daring to travel further. After a few more hours have passed, Lloyd cannot stand to wait any longer; he crawls out of his hiding place at dusk.

Cautiously making his way along a country road, he suddenly comes face to face with a German soldier. The soldier greets him with "Heil Hitler." Lloyd returns the greeting and salute, and the Jerry is on him in an instant. Lloyd is marched at gunpoint to the nearby village and locked up for the night in the local jail. All of his possessions are confiscated except the Bible and the picture of his family.

Early the next morning, Lloyd wakes up to find two Luftwaffe officers of the mighty German air force standing before him. They have come to transport him to a fighter station, and offer him a German cigarette and a black bread and sausage sandwich. Knowing his stomach couldn't possibly handle the smoke or the food, Lloyd refuses the offer. He is then taken to the train station and sent to Frankfurt am Main, home of the infamous interrogation centre. Bracing himself for questioning, Lloyd's anxiety mounts as he recalls the stories he's heard about the horrible treatment endured by prisoners of war in Germany.

The interrogation process is as awful as Lloyd feared. After refusing to answer any questions, he is stripped of his clothing and left overnight in a dank cell without food, water, or the comfort of a blanket. In the morning, cold and desperately hungry, he is questioned once again. And once again, he refuses to repeat anything but his name, rank, and service number. Days pass, and after enduring an exhausting series of interrogations and severe restrictions on food and water, Lloyd learns that the enemy is finished with him. He is put on a train headed for Stalag VIIIB, a German prisoner of war camp near Lamsdorf, Poland.

There are several compounds at the POW camp, and many of the prisoners there are Canadians who were captured in France. Their hands are tied with twine from Red Cross parcels, and from the look of the angry red abrasions on their wrists, the twine has been there a long time. Soon after his arrival, Lloyd is given the same treatment. The Germans explain that they are exacting their revenge for what the English are doing to German soldiers in British POW camps. After a few weeks, the twine is cut off and replaced with handcuffs, leaving sores that are slow to heal. A few months later, these also are removed.

Life at the camp is anything but pleasant. To ease the prisoners' confinement somewhat, the Red Cross sends parcels that contain tins of Spam, cigarettes, chocolate, clothing, and other items. These parcels are the only luxury keeping many of the men alive, as their daily rations are comprised of a chunk of black bread and a bowl of cabbage soup. Lloyd dreams often of the black bread and sausage sandwich he declined when he was first captured.

In January of 1945, the POWs hear the booming of guns as the Russian army closes in on the Polish border. To prevent the Russians from getting their hands on the prisoners, the Germans decide to evacuate Stalag VIIIB and transport the men to another camp. Each prisoner is given a Red Cross parcel and, wearing only the flimsiest of clothing, they are marched out through the snow.

Taken Prisoner

The POWs refer to this as a death march, as many of them won't survive the ordeal.

The prisoners march until darkness falls and the Germans order them to stop. Lloyd spends the first night of the journey sleeping on a coal pile. His feet are blistered, and he takes his boots off before going to sleep. When he wakes up in the morning, his feet are swollen and his boots are frozen stiff. Not having much choice in the matter, he jams his sore feet into the boots and marches another full day. The next few nights are better, as the guards find haylofts for the men to sleep in.

En route, Lloyd develops a severe case of dysentery and the medical officer deems him too ill to continue the march. The German soldiers leave him at a train station with another group of POWs being transported to a different camp. At the station, the prisoners are packed 40 plus into livestock cars that are meant to hold eight horses. The railway cars have no windows or ventilation, and the sliding doors are locked from the outside. Each car has a small can in the corner for human waste. Though most of the prisoners are exhausted, no one can lie down because there isn't the room. Lloyd is still very ill, but there is nothing he can do but endure.

Overheated and suffering from dehydration, the prisoners are finally let out of the boxcars during one of the scheduled stops for water. The men pour out of the cars like drunken sailors, eager to quench their thirsts. Lloyd stretches, enjoying the freedom of the open air, and then earnestly gulps his ration of water.

As he drinks, Lloyd suddenly hears the unmistakable sound of a North American P-51 Mustang airplane in the distance. His heart skips a beat and he begins to search the sky. When a number of Mustang fighters come into view, Lloyd and the other prisoners wave fervently at their allies, smiling and hopeful. But before the men can hope for too long, the allied fighters dive at the train with guns blazing. Germans and POWs alike are mowed down where they stand.

Lloyd leaps for the safety of a nearby ditch and lies as flat as possible as a Mustang passes overhead. Around him, the dirt puffs as 0.5 calibre shell casings pummel the ground. For a moment, he despairs at the thought of being killed by friendly fire after having survived the horrors of the POW camp.

While Lloyd takes refuge in the ditch, the Germans begin to fire back at the Mustangs. Soon the planes leave the area, no doubt believing that their mission was a success. Lloyd emerges slowly from his hiding place, and though he is relieved to have survived this latest ordeal, he is immediately saddened by the carnage that surrounds him. Leaving the dead bodies where they fell by the train tracks, the remaining German soldiers gather the surviving prisoners and continue the journey to Stalag IXC, near Kassel, Poland.

The living conditions for Lloyd at Stalag IXC are not much different than those at the previous camp. Watery cabbage soup and hard black bread are served once a day. Three times a day, the prisoners are tortured by the smells of the meals being prepared for the guards. For some of the men, the food situation is so dire that they hunt rats and devour them with relish. They also eat worms, beetles, ants, and anything else that can be chewed and swallowed.

Even with the constraints of captivity, the camp has a band, an orchestra, a theatre group, and a football team. The prisoners are also required to take part in work detail, leaving the camp under heavy guard to toil on road construction or community improvement projects. Though no one enjoys the work, it gives them all a break from the camp, and takes their mind off the lack of female company and the constant craving for food.

Occasionally, a prisoner attempts an escape. Stalag IXC is a simple compound, enclosed by wire fences. When a prisoner dares to step outside the wires, however, the German guards are swift. For the lucky ones who are caught trying to escape, death comes as a quick blast of bullets. For the not so lucky, punishment is slow and brutal. Would-be escapees are beaten almost to death and then returned to their beds, battered and bruised. Lloyd sees these men suffer and knows that the best chance for his own survival is to simply wait and endure.

Lloyd Kidd became a POW in October of 1942. He is finally released when the camp is liberated and closed by General Montgomery and his Desert Rats in April of 1945. Within a month of being freed, Lloyd is on his way home to Saskatchewan, still carrying the picture of his family. The picture is worn, faded, and bent, but it is intact.

Chapter 3
We All Wish to be Pilots

he heavy Lancaster bomber rattles its way off the tarmac and the aircrew brace themselves for the inevitable lift of their stomachs at takeoff. As the crew leaves England behind, the farewell committee salutes them, and another bomber powers up to follow.

It's dusk, and the tops of the clouds are on fire with the setting sun. Below, the island of Britain is already shrouded in darkness. Blackout curtains are tightly drawn in every room of every house, and what vehicles are on the roads are driving blind without lanterns or streetlights. The land looks like nothing more than a black rock surrounded by the shifting shades of the ocean.

The date is February 2, 1945, and the heavily defended target of tonight's raid is Wiesbaden, Germany. The bomber stream is facing intense anti-aircraft fire, powerful searchlights, and countless enemy fighters. Strain shows on the faces of the crew and stress tightens their every nerve as the Lancaster thunders to the drop zone, swept along in the midst of the stream like a fish in a strong current.

One of the crew is Flying Officer William "Billy" Eugene McLean. Born in Toronto on January 10, 1920, Billy grew up during the roaring twenties, and suffered the restraints of the hungry thirties. His pre-war job was in an aircraft assembly plant, and it was there that Billy began to dream of becoming a pilot. In 1941, he enlisted in the RCAF in the hopes of fulfilling his dream.

The competition was fierce. It seemed that everyone who enlisted in the air force wanted to be a pilot. Billy could understand the attraction. To him, there was nothing more appealing than being in control of an airplane, conquering the skies, and leaving the confines of the earth behind. Of course, there was also the glory to consider. Billy loved to listen to the stories of the dogfights from World War I, and the tales of the heroes already emerging from World War II. He knew that Canadian pilots were making a mark in the European skies, and he longed to be among them.

A Lancaster bomber

And now here he is, 25 years old and flying his fifth sortie as skipper and captain of a four-engine Lancaster. His crew is still considered green without the 15 missions necessary to increase their odds of survival. By the time their kite approaches the bombing site, the target is already a hive of activity. Smoke is filling the air from previous bomb loads finding their mark. Pathfinders are still in the area, marking and remarking the drop zone for the incoming wave of bombers. Flak is booming and bursting with flashes of red and puffs of smoke. German searchlights are combing the darkness, their brightness so intense that they momentarily blind the pilots of the Allied planes.

When a searchlight finds a bomber, it stays with it. Other searchlights then hone in, illuminating the plane so that the anti-aircraft artillery can shoot it out of the sky. This procedure is called coning, and once a plane is subjected to it, a bomber pilot has mere seconds to try to throw the lights off its track. If the bomber is in the wrong position for faking turns or making drastic manoeuvres, it becomes a sitting duck. Even with a quick response, only rarely do bombers manage to escape the anti-aircraft fire completely once the lights have marked them.

As the searchlights in Wiesbaden continue to rake the sky, Billy takes his bomber in for the final dive. Once the bomb load is released, he keeps the kite level long enough to allow for the obligatory photographs, and then pulls up and away. Suddenly, the searchlights find the Lancaster, and the giant kite is caught in the air like a deer caught in the glare of headlights. Temporarily blinded by the bright blue light, Billy is unable to make the manoeuvres and corkscrews that are necessary to break the light's contact. The crew holds their breath as the interior of the metal mammoth glows in the surreal illumination from below. There seems to be a short pause, and then a violent explosion rocks the kite. Flak has found its mark, exploding a wing and sending fuel, flames, and debris in every direction. As if in slow motion, the Lancaster hangs there for a moment, then slips backwards and sideways as it begins its descent to the hard earth below.

The bomb aimer climbs up from his position below to give assistance to anyone still alive. The wounded Lancaster is pitching and spinning out of control towards the ground, throwing around everything and everyone not strapped down. Flak is still booming and banging, and shrapnel from the bomber's wing is flying everywhere. A large piece of red-hot metal shoots into the cockpit, embedding itself in the floor between Billy's feet and the rudder bar. Billy ignores the burning metal and continues to fight with all his strength to right the wounded aircraft. Putting his extensive knowledge of the workings of the heavy into play, he manages to slow the spiral, but only long enough to give the crew a few extra minutes.

While Billy struggles with the controls, the bomb aimer grabs a flight jacket and wrestles with the glowing chunk of metal, trying to extract it from the body of the kite. All of a sudden, the flight jacket catches fire, burning the bomb aimer's hands. He continues to beat back the flames in the cockpit, but it is obvious that his efforts are useless.

The end result is inevitable. The kite is toast, but Billy knows that if he can fight the downward spiral for long enough, he can buy time for his crew to bail out. The fire in the cockpit is hindering him but by allowing the bomb aimer to continue fighting the fire he is forfeiting the man's chance for survival. Realizing he can't permit a member of his crew to sacrifice his life for a lost cause, Billy orders the bomb aimer to leave the fire and save himself. The bomb aimer reluctantly follows orders.

Billy doesn't want to die, but he cannot live at the expense of his crew. He remains at his controls and as the flames lick his boots and orders the rest of his men to abandon the aircraft. The crewmembers who are still able to move scramble to the escape hatches. The ground is rapidly approaching, and no one knows if their window of escape has already passed them by.

Before the mid-upper gunner leaves through the front hatch, he notes that Billy's boots and jumpsuit are completely in flames. Yet despite this, the skipper remains focussed, still fighting to keep the kite steady by pulling the nose up as high as he can so that as many crewmembers as possible have a chance to bail out. As he jumps to safety, the mid-upper gunner knows that the pilot's opportunity to save himself has already come and gone. Billy is quickly being engulfed in flames. Mercifully, the rumbling of the wounded bomber drowns out his anguished cries.

Ready to bail out next, the bomb aimer wrestles with the unresponsive form of the flight engineer. He fastens the flight engineer's parachute with hands so burned they are hardly functional, and turns to drag the man through the escape hatch with him. The cockpit is now fully engulfed, but the skipper, who is a ball of flames, is still at the stick, maintaining whatever control possible as the aircraft plunges to its demise.

Suddenly there is another blast, and the bomb aimer is hit in the stomach by a flying object. The force of the blow throws him through the hatch and out of the aircraft. Moments later, suspended by his parachute, he watches what is left of the Lancaster plummet to the earth and explode on impact. A mercifully quick ending to what must have been an agonizing experience for Billy McLean.

The bomb aimer, who is one of only two crewmembers to make it out of the Lancaster alive, knows that he has Billy to thank for his life.

Many ordinary Canadians fought to be pilots, to soar above the clouds, and to be free of the earth. Some wanted the glory, others the thrill of adventure, and most, when faced with extraordinary circumstances, chose to be heroes.

Chapter 4
Adrift on the North Sea

lying low over the lead-silver ocean in a heavy bomber is an awesome experience. Flying low over the lead-silver ocean in a heavy bomber without enough fuel to reach the airbase is something else again. Croft is the most northern airbase in Bomber Command, making for longer trips, and increasing the danger of running out of fuel on the way home. Those who are on their way to Croft but must make their landing at another airstrip are inconvenienced, but live to tell of it. Those who are on their way Croft and are forced to land in the sea would be lucky to survive the experience, as only 13 percent of all aircrew live through a ditching in the ocean.

Survivors of a ditching become instant members of the Goldfish Club, and receive a goldfish patch to be worn on their battle dress. This is sent compliments of the Lindholme Dinghy Company, suppliers of the safety rafts in the bombers.

Many men flying in bombers from No. 434 Squadron at Croft have felt the knot in the pit of their stomachs when the pilot announces there isn't enough fuel to reach home. All it takes for such a shortage is a headwind to slow the path of the heavy.

On August 16, 1944, Flying Officer John Wagman, pilot with No. 434 Squadron, is detailed to attack Kiel, Germany. Hailing from Saskatchewan, he is part of a bomber crew that includes five other Canadians: Sergeant Wilf Odegaard from Saskatchewan, navigator; Sergeant Hugh McMillan from Alberta, bomb aimer; Sergeant Hank Kaufman from Ontario, wireless operator and air gunner; Sergeant Des Burke from Ontario, mid-upper gunner; and Sergeant Jack Archibald from Quebec, rear gunner. Sergeant Jock Cameron, a flight engineer from Scotland, rounds out the seven-man crew.

The Kiel attack is rough with severe anti-aircraft fire and night fighter activity. On approach to the target, John Wagman's kite is hit by flak, severely damaging the bomber and gouging the gas tanks, causing serious fuel loss. At takeoff, a kite is fully loaded with 8000 litres of fuel. After the bomb drop, John's Halifax has only 1700 litres remaining. At this realization, his stomach hits his boots. He announces the situation over the intercom, and he can hear his crew groan. Not only is there not enough fuel to make it back to Croft, it's unlikely they'll even make it back to England. The best the crew can hope for is to make it to the English coast and ditch the plane as close to home as possible.

In order to stretch their fuel supply, John pulls back on the air speed and flies as low over the North Sea as possible to minimize the effects of the headwind. When it becomes apparent that they won't make it to the English coast, the wireless operator, Hank Kaufman, breaks radio silence and starts sending out the estimated position for ditching, approximately 64 kilometres off the coast. Even after the order is given for the crew to take up ditching posts, Hank chooses to remain at the wireless, sending location signals for as long as possible to increase the likelihood of a quick rescue.

Moments before impact, Hugh McMillan and Hank scramble to the fore and aft fuselage sections of the kite and lie stretched out full length with their feet braced against the front spar, facing upward. Meanwhile, Des Burke, Jack Archibald, and Jock Cameron brace themselves, clasping their hands behind their heads and pressing their backs up against the rear spar, facing backwards. Everyone remains still. They expect the aircraft to skip along the water and come to a stop, as this is what they were told would happen back in training.

However, the Halifax bomber and the North Sea have other ideas. Due to the damage caused by the flak, the kite hits the water without levelling out and splits on impact. As the kite breaks in half at the rear spar, Jack, Des, and Jock are thrown into the dark sea. The Halifax bounces back into the air, swivels slightly, and crashes down once more. Everything that is not buckled down is sucked out of the aircraft, including the pilot. The remaining men, Wilf, Hank, and Hugh, are shaken, but glad to be in one piece. Bleeding only slightly, all three seem to have escaped serious injury.

To order to avoid being sucked under water when the kite sinks, the three men climb out of what remains of the Halifax through a hole in the fuselage. Inflating their Mae Wests with their bottles of carbon-dioxide, they jump into the ocean and swim away from the doomed plane. The back end of the kite is nowhere to be seen; neither are the four other crewmembers. An overwhelming hopelessness envelopes the men. The sky is black, the waves are relentless, and the ocean is frigid. Even in the warm summer months, the North Sea is too cold for a man to survive longer than two hours. Wilf,

Hank, and Hugh cling to each other for added warmth, knowing that hypothermia isn't far away. Praying that a plane will be sent out for them soon, the men try not to dwell on the fact that no one will be able to see them until daylight. They had hit the water at 2:45 a.m.

With their heads barely bobbing above the swell, the three fight to keep hope alive by talking, about anything and everything. The subject doesn't matter; all that matters is the human contact and the sound of their own voices. Then faintly, off to the right, they hear something besides the endless waves and their weakening speech. It's the voices of the rest of the crew! They have all survived the crash, and suddenly there is a renewed hope to hang on together until help comes.

Just as the sky begins to lighten, the men see a half-inflated dinghy sticking out from the wing section of the aircraft. Though it is missing the emergency kit that holds rations of food, water, and the billows to finish inflating it, the dinghy will still help the crew get farther away from the sinking craft, and farther out of the water.

Hank, Wilf, and Hugh swim back to the wreckage and pull the dinghy free. The three climb on board and paddle to the rest of the crew. Then, with a combined effort, the men manage to manoeuvre the raft a safe distance from the remains of the Halifax. All seven crewmembers are riding so low in the waves that the bottom half of their legs are submerged. Wet and cold, they huddle for warmth in the dirty grey of pre-dawn. Each one prays that daylight will bring an Air Sea Rescue plane.

Daylight breaks at 5 a.m. The warmth of the sun revives the crew and the light bolsters their hope. They have made it through the night! Surely help is on its way. At 7 a.m., there is a loud sucking sound, and the largest part of the kite rolls over until all that is visible is one wing sticking 50 feet straight up in the air. The crew stares in silence at their disappearing plane. It's a sad moment, and it hits them hard. Suddenly, discouragement replaces hope. Fearing the worst, everyone but Hank recites the Lord's Prayer.

Hours later, the only sounds on the water are the hovering sea birds and the ever-present lapping of waves against the inadequate dinghy. Then they hear it, a throaty throb of engines coming closer. Four Halifaxes are making their way across the water, and one of them spots the wreckage and the pitiful dinghy below. The planes signal to each other, and all four wag their wings at the survivors. The kites stooge and circle around the dinghy so as not to lose site of it in the swells. One air-crew shoots off a Very cartridge. Another crew drops a smoke float, but their aim is too accurate and the downed men have to push the float away to prevent it from setting fire to the dinghy.

Finally, at 2 p.m., almost 12 hours after the initial ditching, an Air Rescue Hudson drops a fully inflated dinghy, along with an emergency kit containing milk, food, cigarettes, waterproof matches, and four dry flying suits. The men figure that either the rescuers can't count, or that no one believed all of the aircrew could have survived. It's decided that those who are wettest and most injured will don the dry suits.

Taking another turn above the raft, the rescue plane drops a message in a waterproof container. John Wagman decides that since he is the skipper, it's his job to swim out for the message. He sheds his warm, dry suit and stands on the edge of the dinghy, naked and shivering. But after sticking one toe into the frigid water he yells, "To hell with it!" and crawls back into his warm flight suit. The men aren't going anywhere. They decide that the message can't be that important, and if it is, someone will tell them about it when they come and pick them up.

The Air Sea Rescue launch finally arrives from Grimsby at 4 p.m. Climbing aboard the boat, the survivors gratefully dress in the warm civilian clothing they are given. Then, suspecting that the men might be in need of something hot to eat, a crewmember of the launch takes out a can of mock turtle soup. The can has a wick running through its centre that, when lit, will heat the soup from the inside. After lighting the wick, the launch crewmember sets the can on a nearby table. As the soup heats, the survivors laugh and joke, happy to be alive.

All of a sudden, the men go quiet and turn their attention to the hissing can on the table. With mounting horror, they realize that the launch crewmember forgot to puncture the can before lighting the wick. For a brief moment, they simply stare at the container as it continues to build pressure. Finally, one of the men snatches the can and heaves it out to sea with all of his might. It explodes before hitting the water, sending soup and pieces of tin in all directions. The aircrew lets out a collective sigh of relief and chuckle at the thought that, after surviving the flak, the fighters, the ditching, and the cold North Sea, they are almost killed by shrapnel from a can of mock turtle soup.

Chapter 5
Friendly Fire

t is January 7, 1945, and the aircrews of Nos.12 and 626 Squadrons are preparing for a night raid on Munich. Doug Crowe is used to the pre-flight routine. This is to be his 24th sortie, and he manages to function on automatic even though the apprehension and nerves he always feels are still present. His aircraft is a Lancaster Mk1 called *Old Sugar 2*. Fully loaded, she waits patiently out on the tarmac.

Old Sugar 2's crew includes five Canadians: Flight Officer R. Marshall Smith, pilot; Flight Officer J. Ken Yeamans, navigator; Flight Officer Dave Rymer, bomb aimer; Flight Sergeant Doug Crowe, mid-upper gunner; and Sergeant Cyril Lane, flight engineer. Rounding out the aircrew are two non-Canadians: Flight Sergeant Geoff Magee from Australia, wireless operator; and Sergeant William "Bill" McLean from England, rear gunner. Bill McLean is new, introduced to the others at briefing. He is replacing the crew's original rear gunner, who was killed on the way home from laying mines.

The men in the aircrew are uncomfortable with taking on a member that has never flown with them before. Rear gunners are paramount to the safety of the kite. Without a reliable man in the rear turret, the bomber has a blind spot that leaves the crew vulnerable to attack from behind and below. The enemy fighters know this, which is one of the reasons why the life expectancy of a rear gunner is only five weeks — night fighters rely on the element of surprise and aim to hit the rear gunners first.

Old Sugar 2 takes to the air at 6:44 p.m. As the bomber stream approaches Soissons, France, they run into heavy cloud, and Pilot Marshall Smith adjusts their course slightly to 090 degrees. While they climb to clear sky, Dave Rymer reports seeing the starboard navigation lights of an aircraft too close to the port side of the heavy. Kites in the main bomber stream don't normally display navigation lights this close to the target, so the crew is immediately on their guard. Suddenly, there is a bright orange flash, and the kite jumps, sending the crewmembers flying. Doug feels nauseous as air rushes around him. *Sugar* is hit — severely. Swivelling around in his mid-upper turret, Doug's worst fears are realized when he sees that the rear gunner's turret has been completely blown out. There is only a gaping hole where Bill once sat.

Now flying at 15,000 feet, the Lancaster is about 19 kilometres northeast of the main track. The wounded kite starts into a slow, diving turn that Marshall is unable to pull up from. He struggles for a few seconds, and then orders everyone to abandon the bomber. Doug climbs down from his turret and reports that the rear gunner is nowhere to be found.

Everyone left on the plane is scrambling to evacuate. Everyone, that is, except Marshall. He sees that the kite is too close to some U.S. troops doing manoeuvres on the ground, and also spots a small village and a U.S. Army field hospital nearby. Marshall decides that in order to avoid further catastrophe, he must continue to fight for control of the bomber. He wants to give the crew enough time to safely bail out, and perhaps more importantly, he wants to prevent the kite from crashing too close to the hospital or the village.

The rattling and banging in the aircraft is enough to break teeth, and the stench of smoke is getting stronger. As the rest of the crew leave by either the front hatch or the rear door, Marshall remains at the controls, trying his best to hold back the crash. *Old Sugar 2* is headed straight for the town of Laon, France.

Just before losing total control, Marshall gives all the power the kite has to all four engines. This forward thrust carries the aircraft forward, allowing it to clear the town, the hospital, and the troops before crashing into a railway cutting beyond. *Sugar* bursts into flames on impact and finally blows up at 9:00 p.m. The body of Pilot Marshall Smith is thrown 15 metres from the wreck.

The five remaining crew, after bailing out at 15,000 feet, hit updrafts from the heavy cloud cover. At times they are pushed higher into the air instead of drifting down. Most of them take about 30 minutes to make the descent, but Ken Yeamans, the navigator, takes 45 minutes. Independent of one another, the crewmembers bury their chutes in the snow and, following standard procedure, head away from the crash site.

Doug Crowe lands in an open field surrounded by trees. He knows he is close to the front lines, but isn't sure where exactly he has landed. Looking around the field for a way out, he finds and follows a fence line. After walking some distance, he comes to a gate that opens onto a lane. This lane leads him to a small village.

Thinking that he might need to find shelter for the night, Doug carefully scans the village to determine the location of the church. He then approaches some French farmers, who invite him into their home. The Frenchmen call the village priest, and a short time later, a U.S. Army vehicle arrives to transport Doug to a U.S. military traffic control point. There, Doug is reunited with crewmembers Ken Yeamans, Geoff Magee, and Cyril Lane. Their names are forwarded to the Supreme Headquarters, Allied Expeditionary Forces (SHAEF), who notify the squadron that they are alive. Dave Rymer is also located some distance away, and taken to SHAEF headquarters in Rheims. Bill MacLean and his rear-gun turret, however, are never found.

Flight Officer R. Marshall Smith was never officially recognized for his selfless act. Still, the fact remains that had the pilot abandoned his post to save himself, his crew and countless strangers would not have survived the *Sugar's* crash. In facing his own death to save people he had never met, Marshall Smith committed an act of extreme bravery and heroism.

* * *

There is a difference of opinion as to what actually happened to *Old Sugar 2*. The above account has been comprised from the official record. However, there is another version of the story. On the evening of January 7,

Friendly Fire

1945, U.S. troops near Laon had been firing anti-aircraft guns at some bombers, thinking they were Jerries. *Sugar* had been flying so closely to the bomber displaying navigation lights that there is some speculation she was hit by friendly fire.

Chapter 6
Shot Down Behind Enemy Lines

any who dream of being pilots want to fly Spitfires. These planes are flown solo, simply the pilot versus the enemy. The glory, the stories, and the action associated with these fighters draw countless hopeful recruits to the RCAF. Of course, the harsh realities of fire, bullets, ditchings, and death are rarely considered until a Spitfire pilot is on a mission and staring them in the face.

Manitoban Jack Hughes is a fighter pilot in the RCAF, stationed with No. 402 Squadron out of Redhill, England. On July 15, 1942, he is one of many pilots who will be flying rhubarbs (offensive fighter sweeps on targets of opportunity) into France. The Redhill airfield is shared between a Polish squadron and Nos. 402 and 602. The plan for the upcoming mission is for the Poles and 602 to fly into France and, like hounds at a foxhunt, sniff out the enemy at railway yards, canals, and roadways. Jack and No. 402 Squadron are instructed to stand at the ready in case they are needed for defence.

The first wave of Spitfires takes off at 11 a.m., leaving Jack and the others at 15-minute readiness. Jack is out at his aircraft talking with the ground crew when two red scramble flares — the signal ordering immediate takeoff — are triggered.

Leaping into action, the pilots of No. 402 are strapped in and have their engines running in minutes. Jack's Spitfire is second off the line, flying number two to the commanding officer (CO). As soon as he reports that he's airborne, the air controller replies, "Buster 180 deck," giving Jack the go-ahead to fly maximum speed due south below the clouds.

The Spitfires drop down to the English Channel, where there are several flyers submerged just off the French coast, and where Allied rescue boats are being attacked by German Messerschmitts 109s (Me109s). The Me109s are hitting the vessels in pairs, and several of the boats are in flames.

The CO quickly manages to break up the attack in progress, and the rest of the Allied planes fly a defensive circle around the rescue boats. Suddenly, the Jerries forget the boats altogether and turn their attention to the Spitfires, who are now at a disadvantage, as they're in a defensive position.

Shortly after the attack reprieve, an enemy squadron of Focke-Wulf fighters (Fw 190s) shows up to relieve the Me109s, who are short on fuel and ammunition. On their way out, a pair of Fw 109s dives in for one last hit on the boats. Jack doesn't think twice about going after the two enemy fighters; he is bent on saving the men in the water from an ugly death.

Diving after the Fw 190s with guns rattling, Jack makes a couple of hits and then breaks off. When he looks back over his shoulder with the idea of going around again to finish the job, he sees an Fw 190 on his tail, less than 300 feet away. Jack guns the Spitfire's engine, but it's too late. The rounds come out of the Jerry's cannons like red-hot baseballs. They smash holes through the port side of the Spitfire's fuselage and then exit out the starboard side, igniting the fuel.

In an instant, the flames from the gas tank are sucked into the cockpit, covering Jack from helmet to boots. A message comes over the radio: his buddies see he's in trouble and have his tail covered. Though he is wounded and still wearing his burning flight suit, Jack manages to remember his training. Almost automatical-

A Spitfire pilot with all his equipment. The pilot is wearing his Mae West but would also have his parachute strapped on when flying.

ly, he puts his ejection plan into action. This is a plan he has often gone over in his head, but until now, it is one he has never had to use.

Moving quickly, Jack reduces his speed by pulling up into a loop. He is not only strapped into his aircraft, he is also attached to it by oxygen and radio connections. Jack pulls the oxygen fitting and radio plug out from the dash of the Spitfire, then drops the seat, pulls the pin on the seat harness, and stands up. He kicks the control stick forward to create a burst of momentum that he hopes will help spring him up and out of the burning aircraft as the kite throttles forward.

Unfortunately, Jack can't jump as easily as he had planned. The radio cord is tangled on the seat lever. Jack is on fire, his plane's engine is stalling, and he can't reach down to get the cord loose. Crouching down on the seat with his hands on the edge of the cockpit, he leaps out of the aircraft with all his strength, ripping off the oxygen mask and earphones in the process.

As he flies through the air, Jack looks over at his Spitfire, which is entering its death spiral. He then pulls his ripcord and feels the chute pulling away from him underneath his body. When executing his escape plan, Jack hadn't taken into consideration that he would still be catapulting upwards from the momentum of the aircraft, causing the chute to open beneath him and upside down. As he starts to fall, Jack realizes he's in danger of landing on his own parachute, rendering it useless. Without wasting another second, he does a backflip in the air and makes a dive towards the chute. He races past it head first, and the chute flips around and opens properly, yanking Jack into an upright position.

The flames plaguing Jack's gear are almost out, but his hand is bleeding profusely from a shrapnel wound. As he descends from the sky, he wraps his ripcord around his wrist to stem the flow of blood. Losing track of time, he doesn't realize how close he is to the water, and he hits the English Channel without getting the chance to release his harness.

After a few seconds of struggling, Jack manages to release the parachute harness buckle, and three of the four straps fall away as they are supposed to. The fourth, however, catches on something, and the chute starts to drag Jack with the current. Lungs bursting, he kicks off his flight boots and pulls the lever on his CO_2 bottle to inflate his Mae West. Soon, his head breaks the surface of the water, and he gratefully breathes in the misty ocean air.

Pulling out his emergency dinghy pack, Jack inflates the raft and climbs aboard. The channel had doused the remainder of the flames on his uniform, but he is badly burned, and the saltwater is causing him excruciating pain. His flight suit is charred and tattered, and he has a head wound, an injured hand, and countless small abrasions. Reaching into the side compartment of the dinghy for the first aid packet, Jack discovers that both it and the escape kit are missing. This means he has nothing with which to dress his wounds, and worse still, he has no flares to send off to help with his rescue.

Jack pulls his chute from the water and tucks it into the raft for easy access. He figures that if he hears a

Merlin engine thunder by, he will throw the chute out and use it as a signal. However, if rescue doesn't come with daylight, he'll tie the raft to the chute and use it to sail across the channel and home.

With his last act of survival completed for the night, Jack tosses the drag anchor into the water to keep his dinghy from drifting too far with the current, and then passes out from exhaustion and loss of blood.

Sometime around dusk, the noise of wooden trawlers in the surf wakes him. Jack opens his eyes and sees one boat in front of his dinghy and another one coming up alongside it. He tries to stand up and wave his arms, but he can't keep his balance. Within moments, a net is thrown over the side of the trawler and two seamen scramble part way down. Reaching over, they grab Jack by his shoulders and hoist him up over the side of the boat, then place him facedown on the deck. They pin him there and frisk him; they are looking for weapons and trying to verify that he is RCAF.

Jack soon realizes that he is not on a fishing boat, but a disguised English minesweeper. He asks one of the crew how they found him in the overcast weather, and the crewmember explains that they had seen a fireball and had followed its path downwards, taking a bearing between the two boats. The boats then had to continue their sweep of the area before investigating further, but they later located him only a little ways off from where they had figured he would be.

Jack is taken below deck, where a medical officer cuts away his clothing and swabs, cleans, and bandages his wounds. Once he is dressed in warm overalls, he sits on the edge of a bunk and wishes he had something for the pain. A thoughtful sailor brings him a good shot of rum. Later, another sailor brings him a shot of brandy. Jack falls asleep warmed to the bone.

Sometime in the night, he awakens with a start. Things seem too quiet. The boat's engine has stopped, and the vessel feels empty. The light of the ship's compass casts a blue light over everything, and tentatively, Jack makes his way on deck. Sticking his head up far enough to see, he finds the boat is docked, and there are English servicemen milling around the beach area. The boat has landed in Dover on the south coast of England. Jack is home.

As soon as he is able, Jack returns to his squadron to commence active duty. He is one of only a few to have survived the air battle on July 15, 1942, and his act of heroism includes not only his brave defence of the survivors in the water, but the actions that saved his own life against daunting odds.

Chapter 7
Death Before Dishonour

t is almost midnight, and the ground begins to shake as kites take off from the Gransden Lodge airbase in England. The aircrew members not taking part in the night's operations lie in their bunks, counting the planes as they take off by listening to the rumble and roar of the Merlins. These men silently wish their comrades and friends a safe journey, steeling themselves for the possibility of loss. Sleep will be light and fitful at the base, and tensions will ease only when the planes return in the morning, revealing how many men have vanished. One lost heavy bomber means seven friends and brothers are gone or missing.

It is April 27, 1944, and there is a bomber stream of 120 Halifaxes and 16 Lancasters flying in the night's operations. The target for these bombers is the marshalling yard at Montzen, Belgium. The intent of the operation is to disrupt the movement of military equipment to the German forces along the coast of France in preparation for the D-Day invasion. The mission is expected to encounter only light resistance: a few small anti-aircraft guns, but no searchlights.

The commanding officer and master bomber for the pathfinding mission is Flight Lieutenant Reginald John Lane, born in Victoria, British Columbia. Edward "Teddy" Weyman Blenkinsop, also from Victoria, is the squadron leader, deputy master bomber, and next in line for CO. Both men are flying with No. 405 Squadron based at Gransden Lodge. This is to be Teddy's 38th operation.

Lane and Teddy are both approaching the target area in Lancaster bombers. Closing in on the drop zone, the two pilots see the markers left by the other pathfinders. The raid is just beginning, and as the first bombers drop their loads, the flares and markers are obliterated. As planned, Lane's kite flies in and releases more target markers from 4500 feet, redefining the drop site for the next wave of bombers. The raid is on in earnest soon after, and Teddy's plane dives in to drop additional flares, keeping the target well marked for the main force.

About 20 minutes later, their jobs are done. Teddy's aircraft heads home as ordered, while Lane's crew stays a little longer to take care of late arriving bombers. That's when things start going wrong.

The enemy fighters arrive on the scene earlier than anticipated and manage to penetrate the bomber stream, shooting from below and within. In the smoke and flak, the Allied fighters protecting the bombers have a tough time warding off the enemy; the falling bombs and the close proximity to their own Allied aircraft limit them. The air battle follows the bombers away from the target and along their route home. The Germans are merciless in their attack, and the bombers continue to battle for their airspace and safe passage. Ammunition slices through the air, and the bombers are in almost as much danger from stray friendly fire as they are from the enemy guns.

Twenty-four minutes after the raid begins, Lane watches as bomber after bomber is attacked and shot down by night fighters who are working from inside the stream with great success. Seeing the struggle in the air, Lane drops his kite as low to the ground as possible in order to confuse the intercept radar of the enemy aircraft and hopefully save some Allied planes. The anxiety among his aircrew is thick as each pair of eyes combs the skies. The men are sickened by the losses, but help-less to do anything more. Then, straight ahead, Lane watches as the ninth kite in the stream is hit dead on, blindsided by a Me109. All stare, horrified and helpless, as the plane blows up and target markers explode from the pathfinder bomber like fireworks at a picnic. Then the realization hits Lane: that was Teddy's plane.

Lane swallows hard at the bile rising from his gut and tries to concentrate on what he has to do. No one could have survived that explosion. The aircrew strug-gles to shelve their grief and attend to their own sur-vival, but Lane is having difficulty remaining detached. He finds Teddy's loss harder to deal with than others because the two had bonded over their mutual home-town roots.

It's a quiet and sombre group that lands back on English soil. The grounded airmen awaiting their friends' return count the landings at 3 a.m. and wait in vain when the number is short. Fifteen bombers are unaccounted for; a heavy price for what was supposed to be a very straightforward mission. Fifteen bombers equal 105 men killed or missing in action.

The next day, surviving aircrews do their best to ignore the empty chairs in the mess hall. Bunk detail cleans out the personal lockers of the missing service-men, and the dreaded letters are composed and sent off by war-weary officers. All know the empty spaces will soon be filled with new recruits. While saddened, grief is a luxury that can't be indulged at this time. The preparation for D-Day must take priority.

* * *

Teddy Blenkinsop leaves the target area as soon as he receives the order from Commander Lane. There is confusion everywhere: smoke, bombers, and the thumping and bumping of flak. The absence of searchlights is a blessing, but it soon becomes clear that there is another, more immediate threat. Bombers are being shot down from inside the main stream. The Allied escort is having difficulty defending the bombers due to the enemy fighters' proximity to friendly aircraft.

Teddy hesitates for a moment and tries to come up with a plan to help with the defence of the bomber stream. Like Lane, he decides to drop altitude to confuse the radar of the fighters, giving the enemy a false reading on the middle of the stream. He hopes his move will also draw some of the Jerries lower so that the Allied escort can get clear shots at them.

Almost immediately after he drops altitude, his rear gunner begins to yell manoeuvring instructions into the intercom. As Teddy starts to respond, he hears a loud thump and a terrible roar. A force rips him out of the cockpit and throws him clear of his kite, which is now 10,000 feet in the air. Still conscious, Teddy manages to pull the ripcord to his parachute, and while fighter activity continues all around him, he drifts unnoticed to the ground and lands behind enemy lines. He is the soul survivor of his crew, and except for a few minor cuts and bruises, he is uninjured.

Upon landing, Teddy takes his air force issue knife, pencil, and compass from the pouch of his overalls before stripping them off. He swallows his caffeine pills to ward off exhaustion, and then uses the knife to cut away the uppers from his flight boots. Burying his chute and any unneeded flight equipment, he pulls off the rubber end of the pencil and extracts a map of the target area with likely escape routes marked.

As he travels away from the drop site, he works out his location by remembering the last reports of his navigator, and by taking direction from his compass and the stars. Teddy runs to put as much distance between himself and the crash site as possible, hoping in his haste that his location estimates are close enough.

Over the next two days, Teddy manages to meet people who have connections with the Belgian Resistance. The underground plans to smuggle him back to England, arranging for a guide to take him overland through France and then into Spain. But at the last moment, Teddy refuses to go. He sees the effort the Resistance is making on behalf of the Allied forces and feels that with D-Day coming, he'd be more valuable in Europe.

The Resistance welcomes Teddy and issues him false Belgian national papers. Over the next few months, he helps fight the Germans from behind the lines, attacking rail yards, blowing up bridges, and aiding other escaping airmen. During one of his secret missions, Teddy is picked up by the German Gestapo and taken to St. Gilles prison, in Brussels.

The Germans do not know that Teddy is RCAF, and they hold him as a Belgian national who is part of the Resistance. While at the interrogation centre, Teddy taps a Morse code signal on the steam pipes in his cell, relaying his identity to other prisoners at the facility. Eventually, the information he relays is passed on to England, and then to his family in Canada.

After being interrogated at St. Gilles, Teddy is transferred to Hamburg, where he is held as a Belgian national and forced to work in the shipyards. While labouring at the shipyards, he manages to escape his captors and makes his way back to Belgium to rejoin the underground. However, on August 11, 1944, the Gestapo catches Teddy again. This time around, the Germans discover that he is a member of the RCAF, and while he should be sent to a POW camp like most prisoners belonging to the Allied forces, he is sent instead to Neuengamme Concentration Camp, near Hamburg.

Life in the concentration camp is beyond difficult. Teddy and his fellow inmates suffer through starvation, hard labour, physical abuse, unsanitary conditions, and insufficient medical care. In November of 1944, Teddy becomes very ill. The lack of food, water, and medical attention accelerate the decline of his health. Between Christmas and New Years, it is discovered that Teddy has developed tuberculosis. He dies shortly after the diagnosis.

There is an unofficial story that Teddy Blenkinsop succumbed to heart failure after receiving a fatal injection at Neuengamme, but this story has never been substantiated. It is assumed that his body was cremated at the concentration camp on January 5, 1945, with a number of other bodies. But again, this assumption cannot be confirmed with certainty. What is known for sure, however, is that Squadron Leader Edward Weyman Blenkinsop, Canadian with the RCAF, died a hero.

Chapter 8
She's Going Down

-Day. The very whisper of it brings a tremble of excitement and a measure of fear. Everyone has heard the rumour, and everyone knows it's coming. It's also common knowledge that on the day of assault, No. 224 Squadron will be an active element in keeping the threat of German U-boats, now skulking in the Bay of Biscay, away from the masses of invading forces.

On June 2, 1944, the aircrews of St. Eval airfield cram into the aerodrome, not far from the Cornish coast. About 4000 servicemen and servicewomen are gathered together to hear the specifics on the invasion of the European continent. Air Vice-Marshal Sir Brian Baker steps up to the microphone and begins to brief the anxious crowd. "As everybody in the south of

England must now be aware, a most daring and highly organized movement of troops and equipment, which has taken months to prepare and perfect, is very shortly to take place in the shape of an invasion of the Continent of Europe. This enterprise must not fail — whatever the cost ...Many lives and vast quantities of equipment will depend upon your efforts, not only during the passage of the ships in the initial assault, but during the period of build-up of the bridgehead afterwards." The Air Vice-Marshal ends his speech with "Good luck and good hunting."

Of course, for many of the Allied aircrews, the efforts and assaults have already begun. Earlier in the morning of June 2, an aircraft from No. 407 Squadron sank a U-boat as it turned the corner at Ushant. Now, every crew at the airbase will be closely watching the orders being posted in anticipation for their turn to fly.

Among those who wait is Flying Officer Kenneth Owen Moore, a Canadian with No. 224 Squadron. He is 22 years old, and the pilot of a Liberator bomber set to fly defence operations in preparation for D-Day. As the Allied fleet moves in to invade the European continent, Ken, his crew, and many other Liberators will comb the waters, attacking enemy vessels in an effort to keep them away from the invading fleet.

Ken's crew is made up of ten men, seven of whom

are Canadian. In the time they have worked together, the crewmembers have become very close. Ignoring rank and protocol, they eat together, bunk together, and drink together. Ken insists on it, and for whatever reason, the powers that be let him have his way. The crew is a tight unit, and Ken considers his men to be the finest there are.

On June 7, 1944, Ken's Liberator crew are flying "G" for *George* on their first English Channel patrol. Their mission is to guard the channel all night to ensure no U-boats make it into the strait.

As their Liberator climbs into the air, the crew looks back over England, which is eerily silhouetted against the night sky. The moon is high, bathing the Atlantic in leaden light. While the bomber continues on its path, the men keep their eyes to the ocean, searching for signs of enemy patrols. Ken doesn't even think to check on his crew or to verify who is at which station. He knows that everyone is where they are supposed to be. The men operate like a well-oiled machine — so much so that when Ken gets an itch on his arm, he half expects his second pilot to reach over and scratch it.

Everything is quiet at the beginning of the patrol. As the Liberator approaches France, the crew spots a few fishing vessels lying off the enemy-held coast, but overall, things seem peaceful. Ken does a fly-by, banks,

The crew of the Liberator. Ken Moore is kneeling second from right, holding the crew's mascot, Dinty. Al Gibb is kneeling, far left.

and begins a second pass. During the second pass, at approximately 2:15 a.m. on June 8, the aircrew makes visual contact with a U-boat, later identified as U 629.

The German submarine is clearly visible in the moonlight. Fully surfaced, it is travelling through the English Channel like a racehorse out of the gate. From the Liberator, Ken's crew can see the unmistakable black outline of the submarine's conning tower. Inside the tower, seven Nazi sailors are manning the guns and waiting for the kite to get into range. The crew jumps into action.

The radar operator, reading the blip on the screen, starts relaying information within seconds of the sighting. Ken does the calculations quickly in his head, as there is no time for more accurate measurements. The second pilot looks after the engines and sets up the automatic camera to record the attack. The navigator sets up his bombing panel, checks the six depth charges, and sees that the bombing doors are opened. The wireless operator flashes signals and coordinates back to the base so that they know a target has been sighted. The engineer is in position in the open bomb bay to watch the effects of the depth charges, and the gunners start firing on the U-boat from a couple kilometres off starboard. The crew works quickly, as they know they only have about 30 seconds if the U-boat suddenly decides to submerge.

The Liberator flies in and attacks. Crewmember Al Gibb opens up with the nose guns, scoring numerous hits on the conning tower and deck. Gibb also shoots two of the Nazis gunners and they fall into the sea. The U-boat returns fire immediately, and intense flak is coming at the kite. Ken flies as evasively as he can without compromising their own chance of a hit.

The Liberator's crew then spots a few of the U-boat crew running along the deck of the submarine. As one of the kite's guns open up, Ken sees a German sailor grab his stomach and fall into the water. The Liberator swoops in closer to the U-boat, and as it flies over the conning tower, all four engines vibrating, the bomb aimer drops six depth charges down the stick. It's a perfect straddle — three on either side of the German vessel. The U-boat is blown out of the water with such great force that one of Ken's gunners reports seeing the submarine's bottom rise right out of the sea. Astonished by the sight, the gunner cries, "Oh, God, we've blown her clean out of the water!"

Ken flies closer to make another run in, and sees the heaving waters, the huge amounts of debris, and distinct patches of black oil forming on the green of the ocean. In the oil patches are darker spots, which he presumes are bodies. Before the crew continues on their way, the wireless operator sends a "Definite Kill" message back to the base, giving details and locations.

"Lets get another one," Ken says half joking.

Just east of the Liberator's first conquest, another U-boat has opened fire on a French fishing fleet. The fleet, consisting of about 20 vessels, cuts their nets and quickly leaves the area. Soon after, the Liberator's bomb aimer spots the second U-boat, number U 373, travelling across the English Channel ahead of them. He shouts out a warning over the intercom, and Ken makes a weave to port, putting the U-boat on their starboard side. The crew prepares for yet another attack.

The second battle is training-perfect, and almost a duplicate of the first. Lit by the moon, the U-boat is fully surfaced and boldly slicing its way through the channel. The Liberator crew opens fire from the nose turret about two kilometres out, and Ken flies in for the kill. Unlike the previous U-boat, however, this one is already gunning for the heavy. The Germans are shooting a perfect fan of tracer from the conning tower, and Ken has no choice but to fly through it and hope for the best.

As Ken does the fly-in, the depth charges straddle a line about 10 feet behind the tower, four on one side, and two on the other. The hit is perfect, and it slices the vessel from starboard to port. The Liberator banks to starboard for a fly-by, and the aircrew sees that heavy oil is trailing the U-boat, and its stern is dipping down into the sea.

For a moment, the aircrew is disappointed, as it looks like their attack didn't result in a kill, merely a disabling. Ken is about to tell the wireless operator to make the call for someone else in the area to come in to finish the job, as they have used the last of their charges. But just as he opens his mouth to give the order, the mid-upper gunner starts yelling.

"She's going down! It's just like a Hollywood picture!"

Sure enough, when Ken looks out again, he sees that the U-boat is sliding slowly — nose first — into the sea. Someone in the crew remembers to turn on the Liberator's Leigh Light, and the sudden illumination reveals three yellow dinghies filled with Germans floating among the debris and oil slick. And while the Germans don't look too happy, the men on the Liberator are quite pleased. Ken Moore and his crew have had a successful night — the two U-boat sinkings were completed in 22 minutes.

Between June 7 and June 29 of 1944, at least 12 U-boats were destroyed in the same spot that the U 373 met her fate at the hands of Ken Moore and his Liberator crew. By the end of World War II, approximately 781 German U-boats had been destroyed, and more than 30,000 enemy seamen were killed on those vessels.

Chapter 9
Prisoner of War

n July 16, 1944, the prisoners in compound K Lager of POW camp Stalagluft VI are informed that they will be moving. The camp, which is located near the Lithuanian border, is a potential target for the advancing Russians, and as a precaution, the inmates are to be transferred further inland to Stalagluft IV, at Grosstychowo, in Pomerania (a region that now straddles northeast Germany and western Poland). The prisoners are told to leave all their personal belongings behind and to pack only their kits. They will be leaving at 6 p.m. sharp.

Robert "Bob" L. Masters is one of the 650 prisoners who will be making the journey to the new camp. Born in Nelson, British Columbia, in 1922, Bob has been a POW for two long years. He was serving as an air gunner with No. 51 Squadron when he was shot down over Germany in 1942, captured, and brought to Stalagluft VI. And though life has been interminably hard since then, he has been able to find comfort in simple luxuries.

Over the last two years Bob has accumulated a small but important store of possessions from the Red Cross parcels issued to the prisoners. Among these luxuries are a hairbrush, a toothbrush, and a Bible. Like many of his fellow prisoners, Bob is upset when he is ordered to leave his treasured possessions behind. As he and many of his inmates try to think of ways to smuggle their belongings to the new camp, they quickly realize there is another object they must somehow bring with them: the camp radio. The radio is carefully disassembled and the parts are hidden in pockets, shoes, and even body cavities.

A few hours before the prisoners are to set out, the POW camp is in chaos. Only months before, there had been an escape at the camp, and the Germans now have no idea how many men are actually interned there. Wanting an accurate count before moving the POWs, assemblies are called.

Bob is among the many prisoners who organize to confuse and frustrate their captors. They play the shell

game with the guards; every time a section of men is tal-
lied, a few sneak to the back of the compound to be
counted again. By the time the count is finished, there
are more men officially at the camp than were ever
brought through the gates. A small victory, perhaps, but
if the Germans don't know how many prisoners there
are, they may not notice if a few escape during the trip.

Bob Masters is in the first column moving out. The
initial leg of the journey is relatively short, and the prisoners soon arrive at a train station, where old livestock
boxcars are waiting for them. Bob is nudged into a car
with about 40 other prisoners, and the doors are slid
shut, bolted, and locked from the outside. There are no
windows in the boxcars, no ventilation of any kind, and
the men barely have enough room to sit down.

The train arrives in Memel, Lithuania, at 10 p.m.
Bob marches with the rest of the men to a nearby wharf,
where the SS *Insterburg*, a 1500-tonne coastal freighter,
stands ready. The boat's tween-decks have been
removed, and the 650 POWs are instructed to leave their
meagre belongings on deck and crawl below through
the manholes. The floor of the freighter becomes a sea
of bodies; each man is allotted just enough room to sit
with his knees under his chin. For three days, the prisoners are kept below like this. Only one man at a time is
permitted on deck to relieve himself, but the majority of

the men do not bother to leave the hold.

Once a day, a black kettle of lukewarm cabbage soup is lowered through the hatches, but no one has cups, spoons, or bowls, and only a few prisoners can actually get to the soup. The only comfort the prisoners are afforded is the ventilation through the hatches above, which are mercifully left open for most of the voyage.

On the third day, the ship docks at Swinemünde naval base, located on the Oder River estuary. None of the POWs are given the time to find their own kits on deck, but are instructed instead to take the first one they come to and move along. This sparks rumours that the Nazis are planning to execute all the prisoners. Foremost on everyone's mind are the 50 men murdered by the Gestapo after the Great Escape a few months earlier.

The prisoners are organized and marched off the ship, then ushered back into boxcars. The sun is unbearably hot, and the unventilated cars stifling. Bob, like many of the prisoners, hasn't received water since he first left the camp. The heat in the boxcars is unbearable, and Bob soon feels faint.

Shortly after everyone is packed in and locked down, the air sirens sound as a port cruiser starts firing off rounds. A smoke screen is laid over the port, and the train stays in the smoke and oppressive heat until the all clear is given. Some of the prisoners pass out. Fortunately, they arrive in Kiefueide, Pomerania, a few hours after the train pulls out.

At the rail yards, the men are paired and hand-cuffed together for the march to their new camp. The column is led by teenaged Kriegsmarine sailors, who are enthusiastic Nazis, and impatient. The other guards on the journey are Volksturm World War I veterans, who are much more tolerant than their younger counterparts.

The column is ordered to march out in double time. The men at the back of the column take time before they can comply. Once underway, there are occasional pile-ups as the prisoners at the front of the line tire and those at the back catch up.

Bob is one of the few prisoners to be marching without handcuffs. One of the older men is in bad shape after the train ride, and Bob and another prisoner are allowed to keep their hands free in order to help support this man during the march. As the prisoners struggle on in double time, starving, parched, and exhausted, they suffer the added challenge of marching on a road made of uneven cobblestones.

The guards have dogs with them, as well as hand-held bayonets and rifles. The younger sailors brandish the weapons with obvious enjoyment. The dogs attack unchecked, and rifle butts are used to hit prisoners across the head if the guards feel the men aren't travelling fast enough. The bayonets are wielded with relish, wounding many prisoners. The Germans are merciless, but the column must keep moving.

After about a kilometre of marching, the prisoners turn on to a dirt road that seems to be going deeper into the bush, leading nowhere. The murmuring among the men in the column increases, and Bob tries to calm the fear that is mounting inside him. Whispers of execution and a mass grave are circulating. Prisoners begin looking to the left and right of the road, straining to see if they can spot any open trenches dug out in the fields beyond. Bob continues to support his fellow prisoner as they march, but he wonders if he is helping the older man to survive only to lead him to his grave.

When Stalagluft IV finally comes into sight and the prisoners see the barbed wire fence, the postern boxes, and the bleak compound buildings, the faces of even the weariest of the men break out into smiles of relief. The journey is over, and there will be no executions.

Water is finally issued in a limited quantity, and every POW lies down where they are, succumbing to their exhaustion. The trip lasted for three brutal days, and ended in a three-kilometre run. The 650 POWs are now interned in a safer camp, where their kits can be returned to their rightful owners, and their illegal radio can be secretly reassembled. Bob Masters is happy to have done his part to help his fellow inmates. He and most of the others will remain in this camp until it is liberated in 1945.

Chapter 10
Capture and Escape

here is a hot wind blowing as Flying Officer Raymond John Frederick Sherk climbs into his Spitfire and prepares for takeoff. Hailing from Hamilton, Ontario, Ray enlisted with the RCAF on September 16, 1940 and once overseas, joined the air offensive on the African continent. He is stationed with No. 601 Squadron, and on this night, he and two other fighters have orders to conduct a seek out and destroy mission on an ammunition train in the vicinity of Charing Cross, near Mersa Matruh, Egypt.

The three Mk IX Spitfires go through their engine checks, running up the Merlin 70 engines and testing the pressure and drops, the flaps, and the rudders. Of all the fighters to date, this Spitfire is the quickest and most responsive, judged to be at least on a par with its German counterpart, the Fw 190. With a well-trained pilot at the stick, the Spitfire Mk IX is a formidable foe.

Taking to the skies, the buzzing of the three fighters sounds more like a chorus of oversized mosquitoes than a group of deadly aircraft. They head for their target in formation; the squadron leader is in the lead, with one Spitfire off the right wing and the other off the left. Each pilot is keenly aware of the airspace around him.

Flying relatively close to the ground to avoid radar detection, the men comb the railway tracks looking for their target. Keeping an eye on their steadily declining gas gauges, the three are forced to turn back before sighting the ammunition train. Out of the blue, two Junkers 52 dive in towards the Spitfires from above, guns blazing. The three planes split up, outflank, and shoot down one Junkers while the other banks and runs.

Heading for home, Ray switches his fuel supply from the long-range petrol tank to the main one. Suddenly there is an air lock, and the engine sputters. Flying only 200 feet above the ground, Ray doesn't have enough time to recover the engine, and is forced to land on enemy soil. Keeping his nose up, he glides as best he can and uses the rudders to control the landing. The

Capture and Escape

Spitfire comes to a stop, but only after sustaining damage to the fuel line. Ray realizes his only way home will be as a guest on another aircraft, or on his own two feet. He is over 60 kilometres from Allied lines.

After reporting his location and situation to his flight leader on the wireless, Ray is ordered to leave the Spitfire and make his way to the Allied lines on foot.

Stripping off his excess gear, Ray takes only what he needs: his escape kit (with compass, knife, and maps) and his emergency rations. He starts walking due east. About two hours into the hike, two Spitfires fly overhead but don't see him. He walks through the night, stopping at a secluded spot just before sunrise to eat, drink, and sleep until darkness falls again.

When evening approaches, Ray leaves his refuge and starts off again. As he draws close to the Allied lines, he is caught unawares by an Italian patrol and captured. He is searched at gunpoint, and everything except his clothing is confiscated. He is then taken by jeep to a nearby camp, and escorted to the officer in charge.

Ray remains calm and stares blankly at the Italian officer. The officer smokes a cigarette and stares blankly back. He is holding Ray's personal belongings, and he decides to return the prisoner's pack of cigarettes before the interrogation begins. Ray smiles, knowing his compass is still hidden in the cigarette package, then gives the officer his name, rank, and service number — nothing more. The two men smoke and laugh, and the next day Ray is moved out by field ambulance to the Italian Army's headquarters.

Ray has walked over 64 kilometres in 24 hours and is exhausted by the time he reaches enemy headquarters. Despite his exhaustion, he watches closely for any means of escape. He is certain that if he escapes, he could find his way back to Allied lines with the use of his compass. All he needs is the right opportunity to make his getaway.

Ray quickly discovers that the intelligence officer at the Italian headquarters speaks fluent English and is not as easygoing as the previous interrogator. This one doesn't laugh and smoke, and he won't put up with Ray's refusal to divulge any further information. He barks questions at Ray and grows impatient when they are not answered. The officer then tries a number of approaches, asking the same questions in different ways in order to trick the answers out of his prisoner. Alert to these tactics, Ray still manages to stand his ground.

Unhappy with the results of the meeting, the officer orders that Ray be issued a German flying suit instead of an English one, and sends him to sleep on the sand with the guards. That night, Ray slips away while the guards slumber. He manages to cover about 90 metres before the guards discover he's missing. Ray briefly considers making a run for it, but realizing that he may be shot down if he tries, he chooses instead to pretend he was merely relieving himself, and returns to the camp.

The next morning, Ray is taken by truck to El Daba. Arriving at 5:30 p.m., he and a guard are given instructions to hitchhike further on. But when they have no success flagging down a ride, Ray is jailed in El Daba and turned over to the Germans. He is then brought to a tent for more interrogation.

At first, Ray is relieved when he sees a Red Cross official enter the interrogation room. The official is a pleasant man by the name of Corporal Barnes. He explains to Ray that the German authorities require him to fill out many forms, and asks for Ray's patience and cooperation. The fighter pilot simply smiles. The official then presents Ray with a pen and a bogus form on which there are approximately 30 questions. Ray fills out his name, rank, and number, and then hands the form back to the German. The official stares at the near empty form and suddenly flies into a rage. Yelling and cursing, he produces examples of forms that have allegedly been completed and signed by other prisoners of war.

Ray looks at these forms calmly, but none of the signatures seem familiar to him. Of course, even if he had recognized a name or two, it wouldn't have changed his mind. He knows that he cannot fill in the forms. No matter what they do, he will resist helping the enemy. Ray asks if he can smoke, extracts a cigarette from the package with the compass in it, and smiles to himself.

Annoyed at Ray's refusal to cooperate, the German interrogator orders him stripped and searched, but again, the compass in his package of cigarettes is overlooked. When the strip search is complete, Ray is escorted to another tent, where all of his clothes are taken. He spends a cold and lonely few days in the tent, naked and waiting.

It is October 3, 1942, when the German official realizes the flying suit Ray had been wearing earlier is a German one. Ray is then accused of being a spy, and is interrogated further. Once again, he refuses to give any answers beyond his name, rank, and service number. And once again, the interrogator flies into a rage. As the German fumes, Ray calculates the level of threat and decides that in order to avoid being harmed, he needs to volunteer some answers. He lies to the interrogator, stating that he belonged to No. 74 Squadron, and that his Spitfire had been shot down on September 26. Somewhat mollified by the misinformation, the interrogator orders that Ray be dressed and moved to share a tent with another prisoner.

Capture and Escape

The other prisoner in Ray's new tent is a South African who claims to be a lieutenant and air observer from a Halifax bomber. It doesn't take long for Ray to realize the man was assigned to the tent to pump him for information. Ray and the South African are moved to Mersa Matruh the next day. The informant tells Ray that he is going to be flown to Italy in a Ju52 for cooperating with interrogators, and then he advises Ray to cooperate as well. When Ray ignores this advice, the South African gets annoyed and tells him he is a fool for keeping his mouth shut, as the remainder of his captivity will not be pleasant. Shortly after this, Ray is handed back to the Italians.

Ray is assigned to a tent that is already occupied by another prisoner of war. This prisoner identifies himself as a pilot from Southend-on-Sea, England. He is rough around the edges, and his knee is bandaged from an apparent wound. As the men chat, the prisoner tells Ray that he'd been shot down in a Wellington, and had walked for nine days before being captured. Ray relaxes when the stranger is able to give him the name of his wing commander. Convinced this pilot is both English and a prisoner, Ray reveals to him that he is from No. 601 Squadron and had been picked up the day after he ditched his plane. Ray also shows the English prisoner the compass in the package of cigarettes.

Later that day, he is turned over to a German guard and the two hitchhike to Fuka, en route to El Daba. On the way there, the guard demands Ray's cigarette package and removes the compass. The German then cocks his revolver, and Ray knows he needs to be very careful.

On October 6, 1942, Ray is taken to a compound in Mersa, where he shares sleeping quarters with two British prisoners. Ray is not sure why he is moved around so much, or why he keeps getting tossed back and forth between the Italians and the Germans. But, wanting very much to stay alive, he complies with his captors.

The next day, 20 other prisoners join Ray and the British POWs, and the whole group is transported to Derna, on the Libyan coast. Among the other prisoners being transferred with Ray are two RAF officers: a flying officer by the name of McLarty, and a pilot by the name of Trevor-Harvie. Comparing notes, the three comrades discover that the pilot claiming to be from Southend-on-Sea had actually been a plant. That was how the guard had known to remove Larry's compass from the pack of cigarettes.

After leaving Derna, the prisoners spend the night at Lecee, and the next day they are put on a train for Bari, Italy. Once in Bari, Ray is quarantined for three weeks before being permitted into the POW compound.

Much to his annoyance, he is never given a reason for this quarantine.

When Ray is finally let into the compound, he is greeted by horrific conditions. Medical supplies, or supplies of any kind, are almost non-existent, and the prisoners are suffering terribly. There are no parcels from the Red Cross, and many of the men are dying of starvation. Most of the prisoners are forced to catch and eat rats if they want to survive.

Christmas comes and goes, and the future seems bleak. Men are dying, and everyone is struggling to survive a day at a time. In February of 1943, things start to marginally improve. Ray is finally given some new clothes: a shirt and shorts. Red Cross parcels begin to arrive, and they are filled with food, tea, coffee, cigarettes, and other items of comfort. Almost overnight, the morale at the camp greatly improves.

On March 3, 1943, Ray is moved to the Sulmona POW camp where conditions are much better. He soon joins the escape committee. Ray copies maps and fashions clothing from blankets for the prisoners who plan to escape. He even takes part in digging a tunnel. During Ray's time in Sulmona, two officers manage to escape, but are later captured and returned.

On July 15, 1943, Ray is one of 160 POWs to be moved to a camp in Rimini, on the east coast of Italy.

RAF officer McLarty is also among the men going to Rimini, and Ray and McLarty decide to stick together. While they are at the new camp, elaborate plans for an escape are put into action. On September 10, there is a prisoner revolt and a senior British officer takes over the camp. However, when news arrives that German troops will be arriving soon to regain control of the camp, the prisoners gather what they need and make for the hills. The chase is on. The Germans use dogs to comb the area surrounding the camp, and within two days, many of the escaped POWs have been recaptured. Ray and McLarty are not among them.

The two comrades have food and water, and they decide to lay low in the woods for a few days, until the search for the POWs dies down. But their plan fails. Unfortunately, both men are recaptured as soon as they leave the woods. Ray and McLarty, along with three other prisoners are forced by their German captors to begin the march back to the camp. It is a warm day, and in the heat of the afternoon the whole party takes a break. Ray and McLarty ask for permission to sit a fair distance away in the shade of a nearby rock. They are granted permission, and the two men go about making their second escape.

McLarty props a hat up on the rock so that the Germans will think they are still there. Then, wasting no time, Ray and McLarty roll down a steep hill and hide in the trees. When the guards realize what has happened, they begin an ardent and fruitless search for the prisoners, and unknowingly walk right past the pair's hiding spot in the underbrush.

This time, Ray and McLarty are more careful when leaving their hiding place. As they begin to make their way south towards Allied lines, they come across four Arab escapees and a Palestinian. Following the advice of these strangers, the two men head for a cave located near a mountain village. For a while, they live in this cave, and local villagers bring them clothes, cigarettes, food, and water.

Soon, there are over 30 escapees living near the village. On October 6, 1943, the Germans surround and raid the village. Ray and four other POWs evade capture, and a shepherd guides them up a mountain track. As they are travelling, they meet another group of escapees at Campogivde who are waiting to be guided through the lines. Ray and McLarty wait with the group for a few days, but on October 17, upon hearing rumours that the Germans are advancing, they make a dash for the nearby woods. Both men escape just before the Germans surround Campogivde and gun the whole area down. The Germans then start to comb the woods, shooting almost everyone they find.

The remaining fugitives split up into groups of four to make better time and to evade capture by the Germans. Six days later, Ray and McLarty arrive at Cupello, more than 200 kilometres south of Rimini as the crow flies. On October 25, they are guided safely through the lines to Lucera. On November 13, 1943, Ray is returned to London, ready to continue with his duties.

By the end of World War II, Flying Officer Raymond Frederick Sherk was referred to as "Houdis," a reference to Houdini, which means that he had succeeded in escaping the enemy after crash landing on two separate occasions.

Chapter 11
A Heroine for the Allied Forces

ergeant Joseph Arthur Angers is an air gunner with the Moose Squadron (No. 419) flying out of Mildenhall airbase, England. On June 17, 1942, he and his fellow crewmembers are returning from a bombing raid on Essen, Germany, when their Halifax is badly hit over Duisburg. As the bomber begins to burn and spiral, the crew is forced to jump.

Wounded from the crippling of the Halifax, Joseph fights to stay conscious as he pulls his ripcord at 15,000 feet. He slips in and out of consciousness during his descent, somehow managing to avoid being hit by the night fighters, heavy flak, flying shrapnel, and numerous explosions that seem to be all around him. Only partly aware of what is happening, Joseph is jarred back to reality when his parachute catches in a tree. Through his pain he hears the sound of distant gunfire and knows that if he stays suspended in the tree he will be an easy target.

Summoning up a burst of energy, Joseph kicks away from the tree trunk and falls to the ground. It's an awkward landing, and pain shoots from his ankle all the way up his leg. Knowing that he must move fast in order to avoid being picked up by enemy patrols, Joseph ignores the pain and gathers up his chute. He grabs his escape kit and buries everything he doesn't need beneath a pile of underbrush. When he realizes that his ankle won't support his weight, he is forced to crawl away from the drop site.

Over the next few days, Joseph manages to make his way into occupied Holland by travelling only at night and staying away from the main roads. Exhausted and in desperate need of medical attention, he finds a Dutch peasant who is able to help him. The peasant manages to obtain medical aid for Joseph's injuries, and after a time of healing, takes him across the border to Turnhout, in Belgium, where he makes contact with the underground. The Resistance then smuggle him into France.

A Heroine for the Allied Forces

When Joseph arrives in France, the freedom fighters introduce him to his guide for the next leg of the journey, a woman known as the "Soul of the Belgian Underground." She is young, pretty, and brunette, and he is told that her name is Dedee. Weighing about 100 pounds, and standing just over 5 feet tall, the 22-year-old Dedee does not seem like a likely leader to Joseph. He is immediately concerned that his fate, and the fate of those who are escaping with him, should rest on the shoulders of this diminutive woman.

Two weeks later, Joseph is one of a group to leave Paris with Dedee. Following Dedee's usual daring routine, the small group travels coach class with German army officers. To divert attention away from her suspicious looking party, Dedee flirts with the officers and exchanges pleasantries on the train.

Once the group reaches St. Jean de Luz in southwest France, Dedee takes them to her "apartment." The party spends a few days in the flat, which is one floor above the home of the regional Gestapo agent. After gaining their forged passports and papers, they move on to Urrugne, to cross the Pyrenees into Spain.

Leaving for the Pyrenees at about midnight on a moonless night, Joseph's party meets another escape group at a rendezvous point. The navigator from Joseph's aircrew is in the other escape party. He and

Joseph are both thrilled that the other is alive, and that they will be together for their trek over the mountains. Neither man, however, has had any word regarding the rest of their aircrew.

Carrying only emergency packs consisting of medical supplies, food, water, and their forged papers, the party sets out through the foothills of the Pyrenees. Unfortunately, smuggling has reached such proportions that the Germans have patrols everywhere in the mountains, and the officers are ordered to shoot first and ask questions later.

After hours of travelling by foot on uneven terrain, the tired and nervous party reaches their first peak. All of a sudden, two German soldiers ambush the group, firing rapidly in the air and yelling at the tops of their lungs to give the impression they're greater in number. As they run from the soldiers, Dedee, Joseph, and the navigator try to stay together through the thick underbrush, but become separated. The two Germans are in hot pursuit, and the navigator is caught. Joseph hesitates. He wants to help his friend, but quickly realizes there is nothing he can do. With a sick feeling in his stomach, he makes his way back to the rendezvous point with Dedee. It is a narrow escape, but Dedee, taking the situation in stride, is not willing to abort the route just yet.

What's left of the sombre party drifts back to the rendezvous point about 24 hours later. The group decides to wait a couple of days for things to die down before trying the escape route for a second time. Dedee feels that the Germans will probably relax a little, thinking that the escapees will be reluctant to try the route again now that they know the area is well guarded.

Travelling light once again, the party leaves a few nights later. This time, they manage to avoid the German patrols. The climb through the Pyrenees is long, and the men tire easily. Dedee, however, seems to have boundless energy, and she keeps the group moving at a steady pace.

After reaching the Spanish side of the Pyrenees, the group arrives at the Bidassoa River. The river is 46 metres wide and swollen from the frigid mountain streams that are feeding it. Its currents are treacherously swift. Before crossing the river, Dedee instructs the group to strip down, and to bundle their clothes and shoes together. Then, wading into the freezing water, joints aching with the cold, the group follows Dedee across in twos, holding their belongings above their heads.

Joseph's ankle, though healed, is still quite weak, and all the hiking over the rough terrain has taken its toll. Mid-river, his ankle collapses when he steps into a pothole on the river bed. Suddenly Joseph disappears, completely submerging. The icy water makes his head feel like it'll explode, and he shoots downstream with the current, gasping for breath and fighting to regain a foothold.

Another man dives after him, and the two struggle against the swift current for a moment, then find their footing and help each other to shore. Dedee now has a big problem on her hands: two wet and naked men, and no means to make a fire to get them warm. Joseph is shivering uncontrollably, and even though the water was freezing cold, his ankle is swollen and bruised.

Everyone is utterly exhausted, but they all pitch in to help, and the dry clothing is sorted and distributed to accommodate the two who lost their belongings in the river. Dedee permits a couple hours of rest before the group continues on. Realizing that the break is for the men and not for her, Joseph is amazed at Dedee's resilience. He can't get over the fact that this small woman is putting her own life at risk to help a group of strangers, and that soon she will be returning to live with the very danger that the group is fleeing.

As they rest, Dedee tells Joseph about a man the Belgian Resistance refers to as "The Professor." At the beginning of the war, this man had been instrumental in fighting the enemy from within enemy territory. A university professor, he had risked his life for the cause until the Gestapo had finally tracked him down and executed him.

When Dedee finishes her story, the group sets out again, and soon they are out of the mountains completely. Their next contact point is San Sebastian, approximately 8 kilometres away. The group rests again while Dedee leaves to obtain an automobile for the remainder of their journey. Once the vehicle is secured, Dedee's job as guide is done. The group is safe. Saying a quick goodbye to her grateful charges, she returns alone on her 40th trip over the Pyrenees, through occupied land to Belgium, and back to her work in the Resistance.

When Dedee departs, Joseph feels a great personal loss and wonders if she will survive the war. As he watches her tiny figure retreat towards the mountains, he knows that he, like so many other RCAF airmen, owes her his life.

On January 22, 1943, Joseph Angers is reported safe to the Allied forces.

Two and a half years later, at the end of the war, Joseph contacts Major Count Temmerman, chief of the Belgian Underground, to find out more about his rescuers — specifically Dedee. He learns that her full name is Mademoiselle De Jongh, and is told a little about her work with the resistance. He also learns from the major that "The Professor" was Dedee's father.

After talking with Major Count Temmerman, Joseph receives Dedee's address. He writes to her, thanking her for her selflessness, for saving his life and the lives of the many others she led to safety. The pretty young woman had come into Joseph's life as a stranger, but she had left him as an angel of mercy.

"No award would have been too great for the magnificent young woman... For years, she fought against tremendous odds and expected nothing but bullets... She not only acted as guide for allied airmen from Paris across the Pyrenees to San Sebastian, but she ... [also] organized false certificates of residence, false identification cards with photos and false passports. When a special seal was needed as a stamp of approval for a phoney document, she found a way to secure one."

Montreal Star, February 1946
(The words of Sergeant Joseph Angers, RCAF, in reaction to the news that Mlle De Jongh had been awarded the George Medal.)

Chapter 12

The Crew That Refused to Die

t is November 1, 1944, and the Allied aircrews are preparing for a massive raid on Oberhausen, a heavily defended target in Germany. The very mention of Oberhausen makes even the most confident flyer sober with apprehension. Everyone's anxiety escalates upon learning that low cloud cover is obscuring the bombsite, making the operation extra tricky.

The aircrews are instructed that the bomber stream will be over the target between 17,000 and 21,000 feet. The planes will need to dive through the cloud cover in order to make visual contact with the marker flares and drop their load. Enemy fighter activity is expected to be intense, and ground defence is anticipated to include heavy anti-aircraft artillery as well as searchlights.

Among the many crews preparing for the mission to Oberhausen are a nearly all-Canadian group from No. 219 Squadron. The Canadian members of the crew include: Flying Officer Ronald L. Cox, pilot; Flying Officer Lyle W. Sitlington, wireless operator; Flying Officer Samuel Blair, navigator; and Flight Sergeant Raymond Austin Toane, rear gunner. Their kite for the operation is a Lancaster X KB-767, coded VR-U.

The flight to Oberhausen is long and cold. Ray, at the rear guns, feels the chill worse than the others. Stuck alone over the tail of the kite, his operation seems to be a solo act; often, his survival rests on one to one combat with the enemy fighters. As the Lancaster continues on its course, Ray checks his guns, then takes an outer glove off one hand and puts the hand under his arm to warm it. When that hand is warm enough, he does the same with the other.

"Damn cold up here," he mutters to no one in particular.

"We're nearing the target, it'll get hot soon enough," Pilot Ron Cox answers. There is nervous laughter from the rest of the crew.

Judging by the navigator's estimates, Ron starts the

dive for the target drop. Thick cloud surrounds the kite, and for a few moments, they are flying blind. As there is no radio contact permitted, the crew can only hope another bomber doesn't fly into them. When the Lancaster levels out slightly, the target flares come into sight. There is smoke and flak everywhere; the sky is buzzing with activity, kites are being shot down all around them, and the Allied Spitfires are engaging enemy fighters.

Ron banks slightly to adjust his position and dives for the final approach. "Bombs gone," the bomb aimer notifies the crew. Ron levels the kite for a second or two so that the photos can be taken, then banks and pulls up, heading for home.

Soon after leaving the target area, the Lancaster is hit by a hail of bullets from an enemy Fw 190. Ray doesn't even see the fighter coming, but his guns jump to life, sending a string of deadly pearls in the direction of the attack. Breathing heavily, he quickly realizes the rear turret is hit. Panic swells up inside him. He wipes the sweat from his eyes, then looks at his fingers and sees that the warm, wet substance he is wiping isn't sweat at all; it's blood. Suddenly the pain hits him — his leg is burning, his face is stinging, his arms are stabbing. He swallows and tries to clear his mind.

"I'm hit," he yells into the intercom. By the

response over the intercom he realizes his section isn't the only one hit. Keeping his eyes on the bubble for the return of the Fw 190, Ray wraps a belt around his leg to help slow the loss of blood from a gaping wound. Right now he needs to stay awake. With the loss of the kite's inner engines, the hydraulics will go, if they haven't all ready. He's surprised the crew still has the intercom. Knowing that any second, the enemy fighter will come back for the kill, he gets ready to shoot down the enemy.

While Ray is preparing for a showdown from his isolated station over the tail, the rest of the crew is also struggling. Though the kite and a number of the crewmembers are badly wounded, no bail out order is given.

"Damage?" Ron demands.

"Fuselage and tail hit," a bodiless voice responds.

The navigator, Sam, is severely injured. Shrapnel has embedded itself in his back, and most of his equipment has been shot out. Suddenly, flames spring up out of nowhere. Without a thought to his pain, Sam grabs a nearby extinguisher and douses the fire. Although his back is throbbing, he knows he is needed to plot the next course, and he returns to his post. Wiping his own blood off the console, Sam starts calculating their next flight path.

As the men struggle to regain control, the kite dives

and goes into another death spiral. Ron yells into the intercom for the engineer, and for a few seconds it looks as though they are done for.

But they aren't through yet. Ron manages to pull up and out of the spiral, levelling the heavy on three engines at about 1500 feet. As he continues to fight for control, the Lancaster jumps in the air as German anti-aircraft artillery finds its mark. More shrapnel shoots through the kite.

"I'm hit!" a chorus of voices call out, just before the intercom stops transmitting.

"Fire in the starboard wing!" Sam yells loudly to anyone who can hear him above the drone of the two remaining engines and the rattle and bang of the kite. He beats at the fire with his flight jacket, his boots, and his hands. The wound on his back is still causing him excruciating pain, and he is now bleeding from severe face lacerations. As he fights the fire, his jacket ignites and his hands are horribly burned. Once he has managed to put out the flames, he passes out from shock and pain.

The rest of the aircrew continue to struggle in their deteriorating kite. The Lancaster's starboard wing is hit, the inner engines are on fire, both tires are blown out, and all hydraulic systems are rendered unserviceable. After being revived by his other crewmembers Sam bravely returns to his post, plotting a course of return to the nearest airfield for the crippled bomber.

Lyle, the wireless operator, has serious wounds on his face and arm, but he is relieved to see that the kite's radio is still functional. In the rear turret, Ray is bandaging his leg to stop the bleeding. He also is also wounded in the face, and both arms are bleeding, but he remains at his post and continues to man the guns.

Again, the Lancaster lurches forward and dives into a spiral. Ron wrestles with the stick and controls. Seconds tick as the ground rises to meet the dying heavy. Then suddenly, the nose pulls up and they level once more. Ron barely has time to breath a sigh of relief when a hail of bullets fly past the cockpit — the Fw 190 has not finished with them yet.

Ray in the turret has no hydraulics to operate the swivels but fires anyway, as does the mid-upper gunner. The Fw 190 flies right into the hail of bullets. Hit but still flying, it heads for home. But while the crew is happy to see the enemy retreat, the fighter's second volley of bullets has set a fire in the bomber's rear compartment. As Lyle beats out the fire, Ron is able to level out and decides to head for Belgium. Sam, one step ahead, passes the course specs up to the pilot, and then painfully returns to what remains of his post.

When they are almost to Belgium, the kite's inner

port engine re-fires, and Ron decides to try for the English coast. Sam, almost blinded by the blood from the wounds on his face, plots the course for the nearest British airbase. All the men remain in their positions.

As the battered Lancaster closes in on Manston airfield, Lyle reports their location and situation over the wireless. The crew is directed to a "safe" crash landing site, where attendants are standing by. The dying Lancaster approaches the site with two full engines and one feathering, no landing gear, and a severely wounded crew.

Ron pulls up the nose, keeps as level as possible, and slides the kite in with minimum fuss. There is a pause as the dying Lancaster settles on the tarmac, and then rescue crews rush in with fire trucks to extinguish the one engine still in flames. The wounded crewmembers struggle to abandon the aircraft, and are quickly attended to by ground and medical personnel. The men are in shock, not only from their wounds, but also from the fact that they actually made it home.

The aircrew that refused to die are taken away from the landing site on stretchers. After their wounds are treated at the nearby medical hut, the men are transported to the hospital. In time, all four Canadian heroes recover and are awarded medals for their bravery.

Bibliography

Aircrew Memories: A Collection of War Memories, the collected WWII and later memories of the members of the Aircrew Association, Vancouver Island Branch, Victoria, BC

Bolitho, Hector. *Command Performance*. Howell, Soskin, Publishers, 1946

Dumore, Spencer. *Wings for Victory*. McClelland & Stewart Inc., 1994

English, Allan, D. *The Cream of the Crop*. McGill-Queen's University Press, 1996

Lotz, Jim. *A Century of Service*. The Nova Scotia International Tattoo Society, 2000

McCaffery, Dan. *Canada's Warplanes*. James Lorimer & Company Ltd., Publishers, 2000

Bibliography

Mosley, Leonard. *The Battle of Britain*. Time-Life Books Inc., 1981

Russell, E.C. *Customs and Traditions of the Canadian Armed Forces*. Deneau Publishers & Company Ltd., 1981

Acknowledgments

During the many hours I have spent researching this book and others like it, I have come to realize that not only did the fallen war heroes give up their lives for their country, so did the survivors. Many of these survivors lost their childhood and innocence while overseas, and they will live with the horrors they have seen until they join those who fell before.

I have been humbled while writing this book, for while conducting interviews and research, I have walked with kings of honour and bravery, and I find myself very proud to be a Canadian.

I would especially like to thank Kenneth Owen Moore for the insightful interview, and for providing much of the background material in the form of books and photos. Also, the family of the late Lawrence George Cramer for history and service records, and photographs.

Acknowledgments are also due to the British Columbia Aviation Museum for the use of their resource library, and for the time spent answering questions and making suggestions on what stories to look for. Also, thank you for the loan of the World War II flyers uniform featured in the author's photograph, and for supplying some of the photographs reproduced in this book.

Finally, thanks to Ms. Sherry Johansen for her help with the grunt work, and for asking the best question of all: "What does this mean?"

Photograph: Blanshard Photography

About the Author

A mother of three, Cynthia J. Faryon is an internationally published author and freelance writer residing in Victoria, BC. Canadian born, she focuses her writing on Canadian content, covering topics such as travel, family issues, biography, and history.

Cynthia is currently working on her second book for the Amazing Stories series about a war bride who settled in Saskatchewan.

OTHER AMAZING STORIES

These titles are available wherever you buy books. If you have trouble finding the book you want, call the Altitude order desk at 1-800-957-6888, e-mail your request to: orderdesk@altitudepublishing.com or visit our Web site at www.amazingstories.ca

All titles retail for $9.95 Cdn or $7.95 US. (Prices subject to change.)

New AMAZING STORIES titles are published every month. If you would like more information, e-mail your name and mailing address to: amazingstories@altitudepublishing.com.